PRAISE FOR
A Voice out of Poverty

"*A Voice out of Poverty*, is a coming of age story of courage, survival and inner strength which illuminates the human condition in all its squalor and glory." —Vikas Swarup, writer of *Slumdog Millionnaire*

"*A Voice out of Poverty* is riveting and essential reading. It authentically lifts the silence that hangs over the lives of the poor and the severe challenges and stigmas faced by British families who stayed in India after India's independence. I've seen those conditions myself, and Jillian Haslam's harrowing account is full of deep insight about the crushing ways in which gender discrimination, class, corruption, and injustice shape possibility. And yet, we are lifted by Haslam's triumph when she forges the opportunity to succeed—only to bring others with her."
—Dame Joanna Lumley, actress, TV producer, activist

"As someone who grew up in Canada, I had almost zero knowledge about the Anglo-Indian community, its history, and the prejudices it faces. In this raw and honest memoir, Jillian Haslam shares her family's struggles, but also the power of story to help survive and overcome the worst traumas. An inspiring page-turner." —Farzana Doctor, award-winning author of *Six Metres of Pavement* and *All Inclusive*

"Jillian Haslam's story is one of the most harrowing and triumphant I have ever read. Just when you think things couldn't get any more tragic, it does. One hardship after another, this woman had the fortitude to not just persevere, but to create a new standard of what it means to give back. Her stirring spirit is a beacon of much needed light in today's world."
—Sheetal Sheth, actress, producer, author, activist

"… a powerful and transformative read. Taking inspiration from her hero, Mother Teresa, Jillian 'does ordinary things with extraordinary love' and has helped thousands of children to escape poverty through the work of Remedia Trust, the charity she founded. The greatest gift this book offers, however, is the living proof that poverty and discrimination does not have to define our lives and that forgiveness, gratitude and generosity can reshape our future." —Dr. Elizabeth Jordan, Distinguished Toastmaster (DTM)

"Jillian and I worked closely together for three years, and it was clear from day one that she was truly extraordinary. Even so, I had no idea of the many obstacles she had to overcome until reading this book. Her incredible success is in no way surprising, and her life story is as inspirational as it is shocking. A must read!" —Dave Wexler, Managing Director, West Monroe Partners, New York (Formerly SVP, ABN AMRO Bank, London)

"… poignant, sad and at the same time hopeful and uplifting…. her capacity to deal with adversity seems immeasurable…. I am certain every reader will find inspiration and lessons from this hard-hitting autobiography…" —Ambi Venkateswaran, Consultant, Aozora Bank Ltd., Tokyo (Formerly, CEO, Bank of America Corporation)

"Enormously compelling … like something out of Dickens, yet true. It has the power to move with an epic sweep, yet is intensely personal. It is tailor-made for the cinema and I cannot think of a more worthy project to make happen!" —Jack Sholder, Hollywood Film Director, *Nightmare on Elm Street II* among other films

"*A Voice out of Poverty* is a vivid, harrowing, and inspiring account of survival, triumph, and a career in charitable outreach."
—*Foreword Reviews*

"… more than a singular memoir of achievement, but a broader inspection of how personal experience can drive social and political change… *A Voice out of Poverty's* powerful message needs to be heard. This memoir should not be limited to library autobiography sections alone, but should be made part of book and social issues discussion groups, studies on contemporary Indian society, and examinations of the changing roles of women in leadership positions." —Diane Donovan, Sr. Reviewer at *Midwest Book Review*

"Well-written, *A Voice out of Poverty* is a difficult read at times because of its content, but will leave you in awe at Jillian's courage and strength."
—LoveReading

A Voice out of Poverty

a Voice out of Poverty

The Power to Achieve through Adversity

JILLIAN HASLAM

TOP READS PUBLISHING, LLC

Vista, California USA

First Edition

For information about special discounts for bulk purchases, please direct emails to: info@topreadspublishing.com

Cover design, book layout and typography: Teri Rider & Associates
Cover image credit: Shutterstock, Inc., HainaultPhoto
Author photo: Philip Carey, photoruns.com
Printed in the United States of America

Library of Congress Cataloging-in-Publication Data

Names: Haslam, Jillian, author.
Title: A voice out of poverty : the power to achieve through adversity / Jillian Haslam.
Description: Vista, California USA : Top Reads Publishing, LLC, [2022]
Identifiers: ISBN: 9781970107234 (paperback) | 9781970107241 (ebook) | LCCN: 2022939003
Subjects: LCSH: Haslam, Jillian. | Anglo-Indians--Biography. | Woman philanthropists--Biography. | Resilience (Personality trait) | Determination (Personality trait) | Poverty--India. | Poverty--Great Britain. | Slums--India | Caste--India. | India--Economic conditions. | India--Social conditions. | Poor--Services for--India. | Poor--Services for--Great Britain. | Charities--India. | Human services--India. | Social advocacy--India. | Humanitarianism-- Awards. | LCGFT: Autobiographies. | BISAC: BIOGRAPHY & AUTOBIOGRAPHY / Social Activists. | BIOGRAPHY & AUTOBIOGRAPHY / Survival.
Classification: LCC: HC440.P6 H37 2022 | DDC: 339.4/60954--dc

ISBN: 978-1-970107-23-4 (paperback)
ISBN: 978-1-970107-24-1 (ebook)

Author's note:
This book is based on my memories and to the best of my recall the people and places are acurately told as part of my story. The names of some people in this book have been changed to protect their privacy.

DEDICATION

This book is dedicated with all my love to:

My father, Roland Terrance Haslam and my mother, Margaret Althea Haslam

All my siblings, who endured and came through some of the worst times with me, and especially to:

Donna, Vanessa, Neil, and Susan

My nieces, Jillian and Samantha, and my nephew Oliver, for the love and happiness they have brought into all our lives after so much hardship and misery.

My husband for all his help, support, and input.

And finally, to all those who suffer from hardship, poverty, and discrimination through no fault of their own.

CONTENTS

1 | Dum Dum

A bristly, grey rat poked its head through a wide crack in the peeling stucco wall, its long tail draped behind it. It squinted its beady eyes and sniffed the air, as a light drizzle started to dampen the ground.

A few feet away, an older homeless woman, sitting under a precarious building canopy, shifted her eyes towards the rat, without moving her head. A stray dog nestled next to her, one of three gathered snuggly around her, bared its teeth, and growled at the rodent, without rising.

The woman swiveled her head in the rat's direction and shooed it away with a claw-like hand slicing the air. The rat withdrew, vanishing inside the wall. The dog returned its head to rest on its paws and closed its eyes.

The drizzle turned into a light rain.

My mother and I took in the rat scene side by side as we ambled down the street. My eyes remained riveted on the homeless woman. I wondered if she had a family or a young child like me. Then, the noisy "pop-pop" of a Vespa flew near my ears and broke my concentration,

causing me to pull my head back abruptly. I gripped my mother's hand as tightly as I could.

The rain was now steady but not enough to flood the crowded streets or inhibit the pace of the fast-moving foot and vehicle traffic.

I looked up to see an old man pulling a rickshaw coming towards us. I stared at him. His emaciated body looked as if his skin could peel off in thin layers, like a stale onion. He stared at me, showing his single black tooth. I held my stare.

The rickshaw puller veered off the line of his path, forcing a dilapidated scooter that packed an entire family to swerve near us. The scooter splashed mud onto my legs and dress, and I started to cry. My only proper dress was drenched with filth. I now would have to undress to underclothes while it got washed. My mother stopped and crouched in front of me. I didn't hide my disgust.

"Oh, come on now Jillu, it's not that bad!" she said. The brusque tone was typical of how she'd counsel us not to yield to emotion. My mother relentlessly stressed that life could always have been harder. Never make a fuss. Be grateful for what you have, however paltry. Things could be a lot worse.

I wasn't appeased, and my mother could tell.

"We can get it cleaned up when we get back," she added, wiping tears from my cheeks with a single thumb. Her other hand was trapped inside the hand of my younger sister, four-year-old Vanessa, who held on as if worried she'd fly away like a released balloon if she let go.

"Anyway, we're leaving in a few days, and where we're going is better." More parental reassurance about greener pastures.

"Where are we going?" I asked.

"To Mrs. Brown's. She's letting us sleep on the floor in her room for a while. It will be crowded but all of us will be together again."

"You mean Daddy and Donna can go there too?" I asked, my mood brightening. I saw a ghost of a smile emerging on Vanessa's

face as she took it all in. We often lived apart as a family because of our circumstances.

"Yes, but we can only stay for a few weeks, and then we must find somewhere else again. But don't worry, you know Daddy and I always find us something."

"Okay," I said, nodding.

We resumed shuffling down the streets, navigating mass congestion. I turned my head for a long look back at the old woman and the dog. I felt a surge of empathy for her, alone in wet and dirty clothes, facing each day with the promise of nothing. Soon we'd have a roof over our heads in a family home while she'd continue to fend for herself in the unsympathetic and unforgiving slum streets. She'd continue to get wet and dirty. She'd continue to try to survive each day with no family to love and care for her; I felt grateful for what I had and prayed that someday she might have the same. As those thoughts flooded me, she gingerly placed sheets of old newspaper on the wet ground to sit on.

The rain fell a little harder.

That mid-1970s Calcutta scene typified my early childhood. We were homeless most of my first six years of life. Even in the best of financial times, when my father enjoyed full-time employment, his salary was insufficient for us to afford a permanent room, let alone a house. My mother often had to call upon friends—themselves often living in a single room—to allow us to squat on their floor or out on their veranda. When that wasn't available to us, we stayed in tiny, temporary rooms in areas steeped in squalor, where the rent was little or nothing.

Our life was a wandering migration through slums. We were never able to settle down in any one place as a family should. We

alternated locations every two or three months, and sometimes sooner. I suppose the good news was we traveled light. We tugged along two dirty plastic bags with our personal belongings and one larger bag to haul all the bedding we had.

The saddest was the separation. Because we had so few options as a relatively large family, because of limited space in places that welcomed us, we had to divide the family up to make living arrangements workable. For weeks on end, we'd be a family trying to survive as disconnected smaller units. Our vagabond existence destabilized us, threatening to disrupt the family cohesion my parents held dear.

When my father, at the age of fifty, suffered his first heart attack, we hit near rock bottom. We were at severe risk of long-term separation made worse by illness from lack of food and nutrition. We longed for his return. But after his long stay in a free hospital, he went to live with a friend and our mother took us younger girls to live with another friend.

The new family was incredibly kind. I've never forgotten how loving and selfless they were with us, even though they didn't have much themselves and we had nothing to offer in return. It was a brief respite. We knew we'd have to leave at some point soon, if for no other reason than staying wasn't fair to them. But to where?

One day my mother took Vanessa and me to see Mr. Nazareth, a kindly family friend. Mr. Nazareth was a tall, dark, South Indian, Christian gentleman in his late forties, who my parents had met through a mutual acquaintance and in the past helped my father find work. Mr. Nazareth was blessed with a charitable heart. Poor himself, he was always smartly dressed, a habit from his father who had worked closely with the British Army during British rule. His family had worked for the British Army and he always wore perfectly pressed shirts and trousers and behaved like an absolute gentleman.

Seeing Mr. Nazareth was a high point for Vanessa and me. He never failed to have a bag of *Muri Balls* ready for us. Flavored with cardamom, ginger, and coconut, and the size of a golf ball, Muri Balls were made from puffed rice, honey, and jaggery—an unrefined sugar. They were super sweet and light and a huge treat. Each time we saw Mr. Nazareth he'd have a bunch for us wrapped in a paper packet called a *thonga*.

But my mother didn't take us to him to indulge our sweet teeth. My mother sought his guidance regarding where and how we should live, which we desperately needed. He asked us to return two days later with my father.

We returned as requested and gathered with him into the crowded small living space in his two-room home. My parents perched on his two cane stools called *moras* and he, hands on his knees, sat upright on his sole dining chair. Vanessa and I sat on the floor and leaned against the wall, devouring the obligatory Muri Balls as fast as humanly possible.

"I'd like to make you a proposition," he said. His tone was more formal than normal, like a CEO leading a discussion with staff. He paused to emphasize the moment and continued.

"I have spoken to a friend who would like to open a school for the poor in Dum Dum. The area is desperately short of such facilities, so many children in need."

"I see," said my father, with a tone of respect, "but why are you telling us?"

"I would like you, Roland, to be the principal and Margaret the teacher. I want you to teach the children to speak and learn English. But beyond that, I want to offer you all a place to live. You cannot go on like this."

Understanding some but not all, I looked at my parents for reactions. I'd never seen the facial expressions they wore. They were incredulous, off-center, even stunned. They darted looks between each other, and then my mother spoke.

"But why ... why us?" She asked with a rare stammer.

"Because I can think of no one better. You're both intelligent people, and no one could deny your love of children," he added with a smile-filled glance at Vanessa and me.

"I see, but what ... what would the, um, arrangements be?" asked my father, struggling to find the words.

"I have acquired some premises to serve as the schoolrooms. Adjacent to those is a good room—it needs some work—that will provide you with a home. In addition, you'll both receive a salary. Not much, but more, I know, than you've recently earned, Roland. So, what do you say?"

Our parents looked at each other in silence. A few seconds later, my usually stoic mother burst into tears. I had never seen her cry. I had never known tears of joy.

Dum Dum, at that time, was a rural suburb and offered an exodus from central Calcutta where odds of survival as a family had grown long. It was also where my father was born in 1922 to British parents. My parents had increasing concerns for my sister Donna's welfare. Approaching the age of fourteen, she was becoming more and more attractive, making her a distinct target in the unsafe, darker depths of Calcutta. My parents accepted the appointment with immense gratitude.

My parents worked hard to set up the school, following the same model the British used years before. Within months, it was up and running. Using two ramshackle rooms next to our home, the school started with four or five children and grew to around sixty. English was in high demand and my parents wanted to make a difference in the lives of the local Indian children.

Our home wasn't quite up to normal standards, to say the least. The underlying land was once used to dump rubbish and was home

to a generous collection of rats and snakes. We had a single room, sized fifteen-by-ten-feet, in which we ate, lived, and slept. It was built of mud and stones and was covered with a patchwork roof of mixed and broken tiles. Each time it rained, we had to move the old mattresses that served as beds and place old towels and mugs on the floor to collect and absorb rainwater. My mum's friends and elder siblings recall how the large gaps in the roof let them gaze at the sky whenever they slept over during a visit.

The place where we lived in Dum Dum

We cooked outside, not far from an Indian-style squat toilet in a small courtyard—no more than a patch of mud with walls made of rusting, corrugated iron. It was here we'd shower too, scooping water with an old plastic jug from a concrete tank that we poured over ourselves.

It was hard. But we were grateful. We had begun to enjoy our first family stability in memory. We were together under the same roof, which also meant we could eat and pray together in an attempt to strengthen family bonds and let our spirits feed one another.

My father was an early riser, up at 5 a.m. every day—a habit born of his service in the British Army in India. Each day, once up, he'd venture to the narrow veranda to make his first cup of tea of the day and bring another to my mother in bed. Returning to the veranda, he'd sip his tea while sitting on a mora, waiting for Vanessa and me to arrive with our sleepy heads to join him while he cooked us breakfast.

Before this time, my father had almost never ventured into the kitchen to try his hand at meal preparation. In our new circumstances, however, he was eager to do so, wanting to lighten the domestic load for my mother, now that she was the school's teacher.

The kitchen featured a small, single-burner kerosene stove on which he balanced a flat pan. Apart from the plates on which we ate and the one pan for cooking, the kitchen included two large tins: one filled with *atta*, the flour to make different breads; and the other with *dalda*, a hydrogenated vegetable oil, a cheaper version of ghee. The tins were large. Buying in bulk was less expensive and also, because of their size, the tins doubled as places for little people to sit.

As soon as we awoke, we scurried in our nightclothes to the veranda to find our father. We'd give him a big hug and kiss on his head from behind and wish him "good morning." As consistently, he'd turn around, give us each a kiss back and return to cooking. I have this image forever embedded in my memory of my six foot, two inches tall father, dressed only in vest and underpants, preparing our breakfast, fascinated by his long legs, pushed out like a giant wishbone.

We would dutifully take seats on the two tins. We were so tiny that when we put our legs up, with our knees towards our chests, we sat quite comfortably while we waited for the first story of the morning. While the alluring whiff of the cooking flatbread—called

parathas—broke our sleep, as hungry as we were, the kisses and stories he'd tell us are what we were eager to enjoy.

One tale I've never forgotten got told after Vanessa attempted to turn the paratha on the hot pan despite being told not to touch it. My father lectured that bad things often happen to naughty children who don't listen and do as they are told. He proceeded to explain.

"This story is a secret one," he said in a deep whisper as he leaned towards us. "You must promise never to tell anyone I told it to you."

"We promise Daddy; we promise!" we replied in excited unison. I gripped my hands together and pushed them into my lap to keep me still and attentive.

"One day, a very fair girl with blond hair and blue eyes, about eight years old, saw a tin containing biscuits on a top shelf in a tiny kitchen. Below were two other shelves and below them a big pot of hot water on a stove. Her mother asked her not to touch the biscuits, but the little girl couldn't stop thinking about them. When her mother left the kitchen, she grabbed a box, stepped onto the bottom shelf, and, as she reached for the tin, lost her balance, and fell— backside first—into the pot of hot water. Her screams were heard everywhere, and being of fair skin, her body turned red like a tomato. She wound up with a huge blister across her backside. And that, girls, is what happens when you are disobedient!"

"Oh, Daddy!" cried Vanessa, "How did she go to the toilet?"

"Very carefully!" he replied with a grin. Then, he added with a mischievous grin, "And guess who that girl was?

"Who?" We piped up together again.

"It was Donna! But remember … it's a secret."

We burst into giggles and laughter. Immediately forgetting our promises not to tell, we ran into the room to wake up Donna, demanding to see her burnt backside!

It was at my father's side where many of life's questions got answered. He was fond of saying that the best school in the world

was at the feet of an elderly person. Today, I see that as a kernel of infinite wisdom.

Despite our new beginning, we never lost sight of what life was like before Dum Dum. Some parts I remembered and never forgot. Other parts I wanted to hear about from my favorite storytellers, my parents.

So, one day during our routine breakfast gathering, I asked my father to tell us about earlier times, beyond the stretch of our memory. As he often did, against the backdrop of the rising sun, he turned his reply into a wonderful story.

What the inside looked like in our living quarters in Dum Dum

"One chilly yet sunny October morning, a family was living in a tiny yellow room on a narrow rundown street in the city of Calcutta. To the right of the door was a wooden, wobbly chair, and further in, an old, iron bed with hardly any bedding because the family was

quite poor lay a lady who was trying to get some sleep. Across the room from the bed were some old tin trunks with clothes on them and, towards the end of the room on the left, was a table with a tiny stove and some utensils, mugs, and washcloths.

"Outside the door were buckets used for water and a cooking pot, and inside, a man was pacing up and down, repeatedly muttering to himself, 'Will someone help me, will someone help me please; will someone help me, will someone help me please.'"

It seemed my father was more than acting out the story. It seemed he was reliving his past. His brow furrowed, his mind wandered, and I noticed a hint of tears in his eyes. But he caught himself, smiled, and turned the paratha on the pan with an old, flat, aluminum spoon. He then returned to the story.

"Eventually, his wife, who was the lady lying on the bed, gave him an angry look that said—STOP. He turned to her and asked, 'What can we do? We need to get you to a hospital!' 'But we have no money,' replied the woman. 'We'll have to go to a free hospital then,' said the man, 'we need help because you're going to have a baby!' Now the woman stared at her huge tummy and looked even more exasperated."

"What does exas ... exasper ... mean?" I asked while he placed a paratha onto my aluminum plate. He looked at Vanessa and then winked at me.

"Like you feel when you've told Vanessa twenty times to stop doing something, but she carries on," he replied with a smile, and, with a grin of my own, I nodded. Vanessa started to protest, but I quickly shushed her. After placing the next paratha on the pan, my father continued.

"'I know very well I'm having a baby, but I'm *not* going to one of *those* places,' the woman replied between gasps and contractions, 'and we don't have time. My waters have burst. The baby will have to be born here and now!'"

"What are cont … contractions, Daddy, and what waters had burst?" asked Vanessa as he turned her paratha.

"It's like a pain that comes and goes; one moment you want to smile and the next minute it's '*Ahhhhhh!*'" he said, with a mock grimace while grabbing his stomach so dramatically he almost fell off his stool. He moved past the part about bursting waters.

We laughed and then urged him to continue. My breakfast remained untouched. I'd lost track of my hunger.

"The man looked around the room and said, 'Here? Now? It's filthy and there's no doctor, not to mention the fact we have no money to pay for one to come here either. What if we lose this baby too? Just as we lost the other two?'"

That last part made him pause for a moment. "What babies?" I wanted to ask but decided to wait for the right opportunity. The look on my father's face told me he wanted to continue.

"The woman replied that those babies survived their births, but the man said neither of them made it past six months old. She told him it wasn't time to think about the past and to stop arguing. She told him that he must go and see if Jenny was home and ask her to come quickly. Jenny was a nurse who was a friend and lived in the area. The man rushed to Jenny's home and asked her to come quickly, that the lady was going to have a baby."

"Who was Jenny?" I asked as he put another paratha on Vanessa's plate.

"She was not very tall but quite plump with strawberry blonde hair and *big* glasses," he replied, outlining the shape of spectacles with his fingers and thumbs and peering through them with exaggerated bug eyes.

We sniggered, and Vanessa wanted to make this into a new game, but I urged him to carry on with the story.

"She told the man she needed a bowl of hot water and some towels very quickly and then she got to work. The woman who was going to

have the baby was so calm, as though she had done this before, and chatted with the nurse while also dealing with her contractions and pain and telling the man what to do!

"It was shortly after nine in the morning when there was a loud cry and into the world a healthy little baby arrived. The baby was simply perfect and brought great joy to everyone. It was a girl, a *very* special little girl. She was named Jillian ... but we call her Jillu."

Both our little hands rose to cover our smiles under our beaming eyes. We were in awe and shock. His story moved me beyond words, and not simply because it was about me, but because of how he told it, with such love and warmth.

My paratha lay still untouched but, with a mouthful of food and crumbs on her chin, Vanessa quickly put her plate on the floor and jumped up to give me the biggest hug she could manage. I can still feel those skinny little arms wrapped around my neck to this day.

Our lives had changed. We weren't comfortable. We barely could make ends meet. But we adjusted, and my parents made us feel like a family, bonded in a single cramped room by love and devotion. Our poverty included priceless possessions—each other.

My happiest childhood memories are from Dum Dum, and I recall how proud my parents were of what they'd accomplished after much hardship and pain.

The joy that swept into our lives in Dum Dum, however, was not to last. The passing reference in my father's story to two children who didn't survive six months of life were siblings I never knew. They died from malnutrition. Part of family history, it was a dark harbinger.

2 | Tea Chests

Not long after we settled in, my mother announced she was pregnant. As the days went on, she got bigger and bigger, so it was not much of a surprise when twins, Kimberley and Alan, were born. The instant joy was indescribable.

Even before the arrival of the twins, my parents had their hands full with running the school. So, when the twins joined the family, because of her deep love of children, my older sister Donna was thrilled to pitch in and help. And thus everyone, including Vanessa and I, got immersed in the hustle and bustle of having two new family members. Upbeat energy filled every pore of our small living environment.

The interactive efforts of doting on the new family additions brought much deserved and welcomed feelings of comfort, love, and harmony to our home. The arrival of the twins gave my parents pause to see what they had together with us. They seemed so happy, and it filled me with such warmth to see how proud they were of what they had accomplished after so much hardship and pain. They consistently strove to make a difference, not only for us as a family,

but for those in the local community as well. Dum Dum presented the opportunity for them to build and mold something of their own, away from the stress and dangers of the city. For the first time in memory, I could recall seeing my parent's minds easing away from the past and warm to the onset of a new reality: that our nomadic life as a family seemed over.

The bliss of family bonds did not, however, change our financial situation. We had little more money than before and remained undernourished. Most of all, our parents worried about the twins. Although my mother reached full-term, the twins emerged tiny. Worse, they were frail and suffered from malnutrition. While my father took over the teaching lessons at the school, with Donna's help, my mother nursed and cared for them as best she could. But when they were a few weeks old, things took a terrible turn. And, to complicate things, we lacked access to specialized medical help.

One day, I came in from playing with Vanessa and saw Donna, tears streaming down her face. She had baby Kimberley cradled in her arms. Our baby sister looked shockingly weak. I knew she had been ill for several days, but now she looked gaunt.

"What's the matter, Donna?" I asked. She didn't reply. She was preoccupied with using a teaspoon to feed the baby some milk. I stared in bewilderment as each time Donna tried, the milk dribbled out of the baby's mouth. Kimberley wasn't responding.

"She's just tired," said my mother, not indicating whether she meant Donna or Kimberley, but with a distinct catch to her voice. "You and Vanessa go out and play."

"But I—"

"I said go out and play Jillu!" There was no ambiguity in the atypically harsh tone.

We went out as told. Soon thereafter my father came home from the market, carrying a few sad-looking vegetables for dinner. Vanessa and I seized the opportunity to get back into the house. The two of

us, without a word, instinctively followed our father inside. As if we could hide, Vanessa and I sat quietly in a corner, trying to become invisible. As we settled on the floor, Mummy, Alan in her arms, got up and whispered in my father's ear. His face crumpled as he placed the bags down and put a hand to his chest.

He closed his eyes and looked upwards for a few moments, his lips moving without any sound. He walked over to be next to Donna and crouched down beside her.

"Let me take her," he said gently. Donna looked up, her cheeks blotchy and eyes ringed with red.

"But I ... she—"

"She's gone, Donna. I'm sorry, but there is nothing more we can do for her." My father said with profoundly sad resignation and tears beginning to form over his eyes.

Donna looked puzzled and then, as she looked down at Kimberley, let out a heart-wrenching wail that rocked the room. My father had to almost wrestle the dead baby from Donna's arms. When he finally did, Donna curled up on the floor and cried and cried, her body shaking uncontrollably.

Years later, I learned my mother knew Kimberley had been dead a while but couldn't bring herself to tell Donna straight off. She knew Donna had become really close to her baby siblings and struggled with the timing of the news. She needed my father to break the news.

My father let us three sisters hold Kimberley one last time. As she lay in my arms, she looked as if she was taking a nap. I could not comprehend that she'd never wake up again. My heart seemed to stop beating. I've never forgotten that moment. Etched in my memory as well is the look on Donna's face when she held Kimberley for the last time. In all my work with the poor throughout my adult life, I have never seen such raw grief consume a human face.

My father left the room silently, and after a few minutes returned carrying a wooden tea chest, the kind used for packaging goods. He

passed it to my mother, and she placed it in front of her, so the open part faced her like a doll's house with the doors open. She carefully put in an old sheet, folding it to fit, tucking it neatly into each corner, and smoothing it flat. She turned to Donna, who came forward and placed her own small pillow inside the wooden chest, fluffing it up so it would be as comfortable as possible for her.

"I want her to have it forever," is what I think she said, but her sobbing muffled the words.

Kneeling on the floor as if preparing for prayer, my mother picked Kimberley up, ever so gently as if not to awaken her, all the while keeping her hand under the baby's head and bringing it to rest softly on the pillow. Vanessa and I watched intently over our mother's shoulder. I can still picture the baby's pale pink lips. Her face was angelic.

As my mother began to seal the top of the chest in place—methodically, like an artist, dripping candle wax along the narrow edges—Donna burst into hysterics, wailing non-stop that Kimberley was going to suffocate. My father had to physically restrain her while my mother finished covering the chest. I do not know how she did it, how she managed to seal her tiny daughter inside with such stoicism and focus. I will also never know how my father could find the will to pick up the tea chest and walk out through the door. But he did, and in a matter of seconds it seemed, the tea chest with Kimberley comfortably concealed inside was gone forever.

A tea chest similar to what the twins were buried in

The sadness in the house that night was unbearable. My mother tried to tell us stories about Jesus and special children and on and on, and keep a brave face, but she

often broke down and had to go outside, pretending she needed to think about something. We knew the truth. The despair etched on her face said it all. When she came back into the room, I asked her if she had been crying. She claimed she had a bad cold to explain her watering eyes. We knew better.

We staged no proper funeral because there was no money to pay for any plot. For weeks on end, my mother kept asking my father to take her to the burial site, but she evidently never got the chance. People in the surrounding community were most often cremated, and today I believe it's probable my father didn't want my mother to know he didn't bury Kimberley on hallowed ground but had to hand her over to be disposed of elsewhere. We will never know.

"It was nice … she's OK," was all he ever said.

A mere four days later, I heard a rickshaw pull up outside. I ran to the door to see my father walking in with a tea chest in his hands. Alan was sleeping in my mother's arms or so I assumed. Tiny and frail Alan, with his delightful mop of curly hair, had died as well. For once, my mother broke down, seemingly unable to control the surge of emotions cascading inside her. She later explained that in most cases where twins are concerned, one doesn't make it without the other.

We went through the same ritual with the tea chest for baby Alan: my mother preparing the inside, each of us getting to hold him one last time and looking in his adorable tiny face, watching our mother wax seal the chest, and staying silent as my father carried Alan away never to be seen again.

After Alan died, even though I was still quite young, I could see that my mother was hanging on by a thin thread. She was existing primarily because of us, not because she wanted to go on living,

digging deep for the sheer power of her internal oath as a mother. Her heart had been drained. What had happened was too much for almost anyone to bear. Each of us in the family had experienced deep, demoralizing pain, but my mother consumed its cumulative weight. I honestly don't know how she got through each day after the twins passed.

Even today, when I try to talk about it, I struggle to explain what we felt. Vanessa and I, still so young ourselves, had held two dead children in our arms in succession within days. We watched numbly as my parents eased their doll-sized bodies into those cheap tea chests, gone as fast as they initially appeared. The tragic losses so disturbed my father, he barely spoke for weeks, isolating us. The stories he and my mother loved to tell us were put on hold. We knew not to ask. We had no sense of when normal might return or if it ever would. But we could sense how hugs and kisses helped heal the pain, even without accompanying words. We did what we could as children to shower our parents with love, respect, and distance.

Throughout his life, my father continued to suffer not only from the deaths of four children but having to accept the primitive conditions for what passed as their funerals. It was as if he had a constant dark cloud that hung over him. I never learned what happened to my little sisters who were born and died before I came into this life. Similarly, my father never uttered a word about what had happened with the twins, I assume out of concern that it would hurt my mother terribly. I cannot comprehend how hard it must have been for him to keep silent about something like that, to protect her from more pain. That he suffered the unbearable truth in silence shows what an honorable human being he was.

While she was too young to comprehend when the other two babies died, Donna was now old enough to fully understand the death of the twins, whom she had grown to love so dearly. In the days after their deaths, she refused to allow anyone to touch their things

and sobbed virtually every hour of every day for a long time. The pain she felt is what, I believe, turned her into the highly emotional person she became. She has refused to have children of her own and never talks about the subject, and the mere thought of losing someone, even to this day, is unbearable for her. As an adult, I have spent many an hour with people who have suffered losses, but with Donna it remains an unresolved trauma. To her credit, despite it all, she continues to spend her days helping Calcutta's impoverished and badly disabled children.

Our parents

Vanessa and I too cried when the twins died, but to see Donna, our usually strong big sister, so upset unsettled us. Never seeing the baby twins again was something we were too little to fully comprehend. We had heard the word "death," but at the time it only meant they weren't coming home again. My mother said she had sent them to Jesus. But Donna's pain hit us hard.

For any parent, I imagine that losing a child is the hardest thing to face, so how overwhelming must it be to lose four children due to extreme poverty? To be incapable of saving them, literally helpless, after caring so lovingly for them, is beyond comprehension. But the bond

that our parents shared, in the face of the terrible hardships they suffered, was one of immense strength and resilience.

As much as they cared for one another and supported each other completely, my parents also believed that the same qualities and virtues should be dominant when raising their children.

In that first year in Dum Dum, I saw a glimpse of what life might be on the other side, and one of the things I remember most—before disaster struck—was the joy I felt seeing my parents so happy. Today, I can understand that my inherent need to care for people was already manifesting itself, and while still too young to fully understand the death of the twins, I saw the impact on my parents and Donna when this new life we'd dreamt of in Dum Dum was badly rocked. It disturbed me deeply that our sense of peace and tranquility had been taken away, and I understood that more than I did the loss of my siblings.

In the weeks after the deaths, I longed to see smiling faces again. I was starting to find I became happy when others were, and if they weren't, well, I wasn't either. I had begun to assume the sorrow of others, as if destiny held a vicarious future existence for me. If something bothered me independently, it wasn't so important and outside my role. But when others were troubled, I got triggered. Still, I wasn't comfortable when sadness filled the air and I wanted to do something about it. Given how our lives had been thus far, at least the years I had witnessed, perhaps pain and suffering were standard for us, our ordained lot. Still, I longed for change. And change was around the corner.

3 | The Train of No Return

Because of its remote location, Dum Dum didn't include many non-Indians or foreign-looking people, making our presence as Anglo-Indians conspicuous. Still, locals gave us little trouble. They let us live our lives and treated us as neighbors. For that, we were deeply grateful.

My teenage sister Donna, however, with her naturally blonde hair, fair skin, exceptionally good looks (which made her look older), and bright blue eyes, attracted constant attention—and not the best kind. Lewd men had a habit of casting obscene glances at her.

Worse, rumor had it she had drawn the interest of the head of a local gang.

Because of the trauma Donna suffered from the deaths of Kimberly and Alan, my parents allowed her to take time away from school. That meant she spent a fair amount of time outside the home, shopping for the house and doing various errands. She often encountered a variety of men, including armed patrols riding about in their jeeps. At the time, she never reported any incidents, protecting our parents from worry. One day, however, I

was helping her wash our clothes and experienced first-hand what she was going through.

We were walking down the street when a few young men, each wearing identical white *kurtas*, gawked at us with amused interest from a slow-moving jeep. A few carried rifles.

Startled, I asked, "Do you see those men?"

She turned her head away from them, "Oh, they're idiots, Jillu, ignore them" she said. Her facial expression, however, betrayed anxiety.

I must have given her quite the look because she turned to me with evident frustration and said, "Stay quiet Jillu! We need to get back."

In that moment, one of the men, perhaps in his twenties, jumped from the jeep and approached us.

"Nice to see you again," he said, in the local dialect that Donna spoke, his eyes riveted on her chest.

"I've got to go," she said.

"That's not polite, is it? And with your pretty blonde hair and nice figure, I thought you'd be the kind of girl I'd like to get to know."

Donna ignored him.

"Come on Jillu. We have to get back."

I was about to walk off when I heard her yelp. I spun around and saw he'd grabbed her wrist. His smile turned into anger. "You don't ignore me—ever," he said.

Donna shook her arm free. "Don't you ever touch me again," she said. Despite her defiance, her voice trembled and her eyes showed fear.

"Come on Donna. Let's go home," I said. I grabbed the bag she had dropped.

"So, your name is Donna." His smirk returned. "I'll remember that," he said, as we walked away, never turning around.

Donna didn't say another word the entire way back until home was in sight. Several feet from the door, she stopped abruptly, causing me to do the same. She flashed as serious a face as I have ever seen on her. Her tone was stern.

"Don't tell Mum and Dad about what happened, Jillu. They'll only worry, and I don't want Dad to get into any trouble. You understand?"

"Okay," I replied. "But they had those big guns. They looked very scary and that man wasn't nice."

"Oh, they're not real guns," she said, "and if he speaks to me again, I'll punch him on the nose!"

I laughed, and when I looked up, she seemed brighter, except for the disconnect between her smile and worried eyes.

I didn't appreciate the gravity of the situation. I knew men acted that way and assumed the man who confronted us treated other girls the same way, and that what happened wasn't specific to Donna. I'd soon learn otherwise.

Even though they didn't speak the local language, Bengali fluently, our parents had cultivated good relationships with the parents of their pupils, as well as others who lived near us. One night two village men came unannounced to our home. They wouldn't identify themselves out of fear of retribution. They got straight to the point.

They told my father about a plot by the local militia group to kidnap Donna, stressing that the plotters would stop at nothing to take Donna as part of their militia. They warned my parents to not utter a word about it and act as if all were normal. Attracting undue attention risked my whole family being killed. The local gang had earned a reputation for murder.

Our parents were between a rock and hard place. Donna couldn't stay. That much was certain. They could send her back to school in Calcutta or hide her somewhere. But that meant putting us all at risk, certainly my parents. If the family stayed and sent Donna away, Vanessa and I were at risk of being kidnapped. Nor could we rely on

local police for protection. They'd never interfere for fear of putting their own families in jeopardy. The local gangs had a tight grip on local law enforcement.

We had to move from Dum Dum. We'd take nothing material with us, such as we had. More devastating, we had to leave behind something more profound: The twins. We could no longer be close to them. And left too, of course, was all the hard work and effort of my parents to build a home and a school. We were abandoning a life.

My parents, as they tended to be, were stoic, masking the pain they felt. In truth, the decision to leave crushed them. We were regressing to depressing poverty. Donna was torn up at the thought of leaving them in Dum Dum; worse still, she felt guilty for why we had to leave.

Our parents didn't tell us about the kidnapping plot at the time. Years later, when my mother recounted the story to Vanessa and me, she trembled and cried, telling us what it was like for her. She stayed up all night and prayed that the evil men wouldn't wipe out the family in our respective beds. She never forgot the trembling she endured worrying about the possibility that someone might inform the plotters about our planned departure.

I remember the night we fled vividly. Our mother rustled Vanessa and me out of deep sleep about 2 a.m., in intense darkness, with no candles lit. She told us to get out of bed and dress quickly—and in absolute silence. It was exceptionally scary.

Naturally, we wanted to know what was happening. She said she'd tell us later. She then left us hurriedly to speak with Donna. She, too, was in the dark about what was really happening.

No stars were visible in the sky and the moon was nowhere to be found.

As soon as our eyes became accustomed to the darkness, not knowing the danger we faced, Vanessa and I became exhilarated by the mystery of the situation, as if the family was in the throes

of a secret mission. Then, like damp fingers on a candle flame, any sense of fun got snuffed out. When our mother returned to see if we were ready, even at my young age, I could sense her edginess. When she fastened the buttons on the front of my dress, her hands shook wildly. I looked at Vanessa to see if she felt the same way. Her frozen face and uncharacteristic stillness gave the answer.

We followed our mother across the room and Vanessa started whimpering. She grabbed my dress and moved behind me. By the door, like prison guards, two strange men flanked our father. With dark skin and clothes, we could only make out the shapes of their bodies. The whites of their eyes peered at us like cats in an alleyway. My dad came towards us and gingerly dropped to one knee and let out a breath.

"Don't worry girls. These men are here to help us. We have to go away, and we have to do it very quietly. Okay?"

"Yes, Daddy," we both replied. I'm sure our looks of confusion suggested differently.

At that moment, the cloud cover over the moon lifted momentarily, sending slivers of dim light through the gaps in the shutters and old sheets we used as curtains. The lighting gave us another surprise. Vanessa and I wore our normal light cotton dresses, and for some reason, Donna wore an Indian outfit and headscarf. She was also sniffling.

Vanessa asked why Donna was dressed the way she was and why she was crying. My parents hushed her.

When we were set to leave, our parents, themselves dressed in dark clothing, gave us plastic bottles filled with boiled water. We were to carry nothing else. But what did we have to carry? We weren't leaving anything behind. We had no toys to speak of or cherished keepsakes. As we stood by the door, my mother squatted near us and took one of our hands in each of hers. One at a time, she looked us in the eyes. She was otherwise expressionless.

"You two hold hands and don't let go. No matter what happens, just hold on tight." She turned more towards me. "Jillu, look after Vanu and if I say run, I mean *run*. Do not look back and don't stop."

"But what's happening, Mummy?" I asked, fighting a powerful swell of anxiety and rush of tears. "What's the matter with Donna?"

She raised a single finger and pressed it gently to my trembling lips. As she spoke, her eyes darted from side to side in nervous watchfulness, half-filled with tears.

"Not now, Jillu. I'll explain later. Donna will be fine. All I need you to know is that, whatever happens, your father and I love you very much and always will. I need you to promise me you *will* run if I say so. Don't worry about where to go, just keep running. Can you do that?"

I nodded and looked at Vanessa, her face consumed with worry. My mother's words terrified me, partly because I couldn't understand why she wanted us to run away and also because I had never seen my parents so tense. The seriousness of the situation was obvious, but neither Vanessa nor I, as young children, could fathom what could compel us to take flight as we were. Mum told us to take a pee before we left, and as I squatted over the toilet, I shook so much I splashed both my feet.

The two local men, in their forties, led the way. I learned later they were the men who originally warned my father about the plot to abduct Donna. Like our parents, they wore dark clothes as opposed to the regular Indian dress for men in the area: long, pale color kurta shirts and *lungis*, the working-class casual pants. Then came Donna, followed by Vanessa and me, and finally, our parents. As we moved away from our home and the school, the cloud cover returned and all I could see was the vague shape of Donna's shoulders. She was several feet in front of us. I could hear her crying, and between sniffs she muttered: "I should never have come home to help. I should have stayed at school." The poor thing was carrying the full weight of the circumstances on her shoulders.

As we crossed the edge of a field, close to some dense woods, the howl of a dog shattered the stillness of the night so much it stopped Vanessa and me in our tracks in fear.

"It's Okay, girls. Keep going," whispered our mother behind us. "Hurry along as quietly and quickly as you can. Just follow Donna; Daddy and I are right behind you." The softness of her voice gave me some comfort.

Vanessa and I scurried along over the uneven surface as fast as our little feet could carry us and gripped each other's hands tightly. I can still feel Vanessa's hand trembling in mine as I tried to comfort her. Away from any housing, the darkness consumed us. It was all we could do to keep Donna's outfit in sight. At times, we must have slowed down because my mother gently pushed the back of my head as if to say, "Keep going."

We crossed another couple of fields. Despite the urging of our mother, the combination of Donna's faster pace and how often Vanessa and I stopped to make sure our parents were close behind, the separation between us increased. The more distance between us, the more afraid we'd become, and we'd start to cry.

We arrived at a narrow track. We were about to step out onto it when someone pushed me to the ground and put a hand over my mouth. I wanted to scream. But I realized it was my mother, urging me with her eyes and shakes of her head to be quiet.

In the distance, we could hear the rumble of a noisy engine, like a patrol jeep. Lights appeared and the twin beams picked out the two ruts where other vehicles had driven along the track after the rain. The light reflected in its eyes, and then an old truck rumbled by with someone's furniture tied down on the back. My heart raced. Our front men took us down the track until we came upon two cycle rickshaws. The two men put Vanessa and me inside one.

"Where are we going, Daddy?" I asked, terrified that Vanessa and I would end up on our own.

"Shush, Jillu," he said, "we're going to the railway station, but you must keep quiet."

My father and one of the men joined us in the rickshaw. My mother, Donna, and the other man got into the other rickshaw. We headed down the dirt track. I remember clinging to my father like my life depended on it. Vanessa's nails squeezed my hand so tightly it became painful. I pushed the pain aside. We bumped around until we arrived at the local railway station. In light of the lateness of the hour, it was mostly deserted. An old steam train stood at the platform with its huge pipe swinging across on ropes, ready to fill up the engine's water tanks.

My father bought tickets and we hurried aboard. As we did, I watched him shake the hands of the two men who helped us, grasping their arms tightly in gratitude. In a flash, the two men disappeared amid the billowing engine smoke as the train pulled away. I was too young then to understand the gravity of it all, but later learned that if the gang ever found out those men helped us, death would have instantly come to them and their families. I never heard what happened to them and I prayed for them to live a long productive life. I will always be grateful for those two kindhearted and brave souls who risked their lives to save ours.

We were leaving Dum Dum behind. We lived in a harsh and unforgiving country. Our situation might almost seem like that of the von Trapp family in *The Sound of Music*, but, unlike them, we were completely poverty-stricken and had nothing apart from the clothes on our bodies, a little plastic bag with some fruit, and two tiny frocks that belonged to Kimberley and Alan.

We arrived at the next station. My father consulted a tatty timetable attached to a wooden board and announced we'd have a several-hour wait for the next train. Our mother became immediately anxious. She feared the gang members might catch us as we lingered at the station with no cover or anywhere to go. She hustled us into

a ramshackle waiting room, herding us into a dark corner to attract the least possible attention. Vanessa and I, and perhaps Donna too, never knew then that the slightest recognition could be fatal. Sitting on the dirty floor, reeking of urine, we huddled behind our parents until, eventually, we fell to sleep for a short while.

Early the next morning, we boarded the train to Calcutta. When we arrived, hundreds of people littered the long platform, pushing and shoving in their desire to get into the city. In the brightness of day, despite the attempts to cover her, Donna's tears were more than prominent, and her fair skin stood out like a beacon to the local men, who immediately fought to get close enough to touch her. It was disgusting.

As instructed, Vanessa and I held onto our mother's skirt, burying our heads here to create the illusion that if we could not see other people, they could not see us. We'd been allowed a quick visit to what might pass for a toilet and then, afraid, exhausted, and hungry, we were crammed into the corner of another third-class carriage of a commuter train. At least we did not have to hang on the outside of the train, as some did. The temperature was around forty degrees Celsius and the pressure of bodies, all pungent with perspiration, various Indian spices, and oils, was suffocating.

Despite the vile attention she was receiving, Donna focused on helping our parents protect Vanessa and me, who, in the crush, resembled two tiny saplings in a dense forest. With only a few wooden bench seats, most people stood or sat on the floor, and bales of straw and bundles of wrapped-up clothes cluttered the floor of the carriage. There were vegetables, food and hot tea, and tatty, smelly chickens, squawking in baskets.

I looked up at Donna. Tears rolled down her cheeks. I grabbed her hand, wishing I could help stop her crying. She tried to make space for us to breathe, while my mother sought to shield her while keeping an eye on me and Vanessa. I was wondering why

people wanted to be so horrid to us when, all of a sudden, things got worse.

We finally boarded the train. As we did, I turned away from Donna and noticed my father struggling to speak, his confused words lost in the surrounding noise and commotion. Then he started rubbing his eyes and shaking his head, his face filled with panic. Seeing his distress, my mother asked him to repeat what he'd said. I was able to make out the words. "My … my eyesight's gone. I, I can't … can't see a thing."

4 | Howrah Horrors

Despite a face frozen in horror, my mother quickly reached up to my father's six-foot-two frame and grabbed his shirt by the shoulder with one hand to steady him, while holding onto me with the other. Donna, Vanessa, and I had different expressions of shock. My mother pulled him close. All eyes were on my father. His head down, he looked pale and distressed. He began to tremble.

"You can't see anything at all?" My mother asked.

He nodded. I had never seen him look so panicked. I can't imagine what it felt like, with everything else beating down on us. What was his breaking point? When would all the pain and horror become too much to shoulder? His face started to crumple like a child's. He was weakening before our eyes.

My mother's face went from panic to indomitably steady. While my father was the family disciplinarian, she was the family rock—a survivor no matter what misery she faced. In seconds, she took charge.

"Okay, Ronnie, listen to me. There is nothing we can do now. This is something we can get through. I'm sure it will come back as quickly as you lost it. Right now, we are almost there. We have to get

everyone to their destinations. I'll hold onto you, Okay? Try not to worry. Just do as I say."

He nodded. His face relaxed a little, although he still looked shell-shocked. Donna seemed shocked as well, not even swatting away errant hands, as men brushed up against her. Vanessa started to cry and I tried to grab my father's hand. My mother pushed me back down.

"Not now Jillu. Remember, whatever happens, you and Vanessa, must not let go of my skirt." We huddled together. We were a frightened and stunned bunch.

Howrah station where my father lost his eyesight

Not long later, what must have seemed interminable for my father, the train arrived at Howrah station in Calcutta. The crescendo of squealing brakes cued everyone in the packed cars to pour off the train in droves, melding into a human stampede onto the platform. It was madness. We were in the epicenter of a human explosion, as hundreds upon hundreds of people, mostly men, began pushing and shoving to get out of the carriage, as if their lives depended on escaping quickly into the city.

Like an onslaught of rats in a sewer, heaving and sweating bodies pressed all around us, crushing Vanessa and me in the melee. People pushed us out of the way, kicked our legs, and trampled on our feet. My mother kept her hand firmly on my father's back, holding in her fist a screwed-up portion of his dirty, wet shirt, guiding him forward, and raising on her toes as high as she could—she was five-one to his six-two—as she tried to comfort him with words of encouragement while we all struggled towards the doorway of the train. We each tried to look out for the other but were petrified of losing our grip and getting swept away and trampled upon.

The surge of the crowd carried us towards the carriage doorway and our mother did her best to protect us all, pouring with perspiration. She continually shouted to us that, whatever happened, we should not let go of her skirt. Never have I held onto something so tightly. Never have I felt so panicked. My mother continued to push my father forward, navigating a raging sea of humanity sweeping us across the platform.

Despite her herculean efforts, in a moment's distraction, my mother lost her grip on my father's shirt and he vanished into the crowd, sucked into the midst of thousands—half trying to leave the station and the other half seeking to gain entry to the train. Then, as we wildly looked around to find our father, we lost track of Donna too, engulfed by hordes of lecherous men, all grabbing at her outfit and what it covered.

We were collectively in the deepest panic imaginable.

We had abandoned our home and the better life we had in the middle of the night to save Donna and keep the family together. Our exit plan had gone terribly wrong.

Vanessa and I clung desperately to our mother as she pushed her way into the crowd in the direction that Donna had gone, screaming her name, as her head bobbed in and out of visibility among a sandwich of bodies, like a chicken bouncing in a basket.

"Mummy!" yelled Vanessa, pointing a grubby finger. "Over there!"

I looked in that direction and saw Donna, her top torn in several places and her face smudged where she'd rubbed her tears with hands made filthy from the waiting room and train floors. We caught up to her.

"Mum! I saw Dad! This way!" Donna shouted.

Collectively, hanging on to each other, we fought through the mass of rushing travelers, knowing our father was totally lost and helpless and probably terrified. As we rushed along the platform, desperate to get through the crowds, Vanessa and I did our best to hold on to our mother's skirt as she frantically sought to reach our father. Then, above all the tumultuous commotion of people yelling and the noise of trains stopping and starting, I heard Mummy scream.

"Ronnie! Stop!"

I saw my father. He looked like a terrified, lost child, white as a sheet, and was about to walk off the edge of the platform as a train approached. We girls all yelled, "*Daddy!*" and our mother screeched his name again. By some miracle, while he was literally inches from the platform edge, my father heard us and stopped. Pushing people aside with a strength that belied her petite size, and doubtless fueled by extraordinary doses of adrenaline, our mother forced her way through and grabbed the back of his shirt, yanking him from danger.

I don't know how long Donna and my father were lost to us. It might have only been ten to fifteen minutes. But it was the most fear I had ever experienced. It was emotional bedlam, something I'd never felt before or since. Our family intact, I felt a surge within, and began to cry. We all began to cry. We clung to one another, our faces smudged and clothes filthy. I turned to Vanessa, and her normally pale face had turned bright red beneath the war paint of dirt, a mix of fear and utter confusion. Then I noticed the pain in my feet, and I looked down. Squeezed inside our open-toed brown sandals, mine and Vanessa's toes were red and swollen where they had been stomped on so many times.

I cannot re-live this without feeling pain for my mother, my father, and my siblings in different ways. I remain hugely apprehensive about being anywhere near milling crowds. All Vanessa recalls today is the horror of the experience, especially the moment we saw our father seconds from death. Donna refuses to speak about it.

My mother held onto my father, saying she would never leave him. Donna held my mother, while Vanessa hugged one of my father's legs with one hand, trying to pull me close with the other as though terrified of losing me. We had arrived in Calcutta with no money, no food, and nowhere to go—and my father without eyesight.

The roles of my parents in minutes reversed. My mother uncharacteristically began to panic, bemoaning that any accessible free hospitals would be overwhelmed and lacking the capacity to help my father. My father became calm, perhaps resigned to his fate. He responded in a subdued almost matter-of-fact tone that the family should take him to the Salvation Army, which took care of ex-servicemen.

My father joined the British Army's North Staffordshire Regiment in 1941 at the age of nineteen and a year later Paiforce (the Persian and Iraqi command), serving overseas in the Middle East. In October 1944, as Warrant Officer, he was transferred to the Royal Army Service Corps, responsible for providing supplies to various military units. I remembered he once proudly showed us his certificate of exemplary service, which I have to this day. When World War II ended in 1945, my father remained in the military until July 1947, when India declared its independence from British rule.

His presence of mind and smart suggestion relaxed my mother, which relaxed the rest of us. We took a break and sat on a bench to come to terms with what we faced. The Salvation Army was hours

away. My mother insisted we spend a few rupees to take a tram part of the way.

En route, we stopped to leave Donna with a family friend Mrs. Jenkins who graciously agreed to take care of her. I would learn when older that Donna would not have been safe where my mother was taking the rest of us, although she wasn't safe where she had been placed either. After fighting so hard to keep the family together, and with all we'd been through recently, it was painful to say goodbye. Our mother insisted it was best and our focus should be caring for our father. It didn't feel right to me. It was as if we were abandoning Donna. I wanted us all to stay together come what may. That separation would induce a trauma inside of me that never dissolved. I get anxious and unsettled whenever I have to say goodbye to someone or when someone I hold dear leaves my life.

"But Mummy," I urged, "how will we know if Donna is Okay? She's been crying so much, and everyone's been so horrible to her and I want it to stop." Donna replied, not my mother.

"Listen you," she said. She squatted down to my level, swiftly rubbed her tears, and wiped her nose with the back of her hand. "We've had to live like this before. I'll be fine and we'll all be safe and together very soon, so that's all that matters. Some nice people will look after Daddy, and I want you to look after Mummy and Vanu. Can you do that for me?"

I looked into her tear-ravaged face and, despite her attempt to smile, she could not hide the terrible sadness in her eyes. My sniff matched hers and I nodded, unable to find words.

"That's a good girl, Jillu, and as soon as Mummy has found you somewhere to stay, I'll come and visit. Okay?"

I nodded again and managed to say goodbye to her. The rest of us set off to find the Salvation Army. When we arrived, we each were at the point of exhaustion. The Salvation Army was a cluster of buildings in a small mud compound that resembled an army barracks.

They took my father to a dormitory with about twenty beds in two rows on either side of the room. Each man had a bed and a small side table, and at the end of the dormitory, were shower cubicles, lavatories, and lockers where the men could keep their clothes and other belongings.

My mother described to the hospital staff my father's military background and what had happened to him on the train trip. They told her we could leave him in their hands until he had improved. They would look after and provide him with the medication and everything he needed, free of charge. For that, I shall be eternally grateful.

We waited until a doctor from a nearby hospital could see my father. The diagnosis was that my father had suffered another minor heart attack that, owing to the stress of our escape, in turn, robbed him of his sight. The doctor said his blindness was temporary, a major relief. The longer-term worry was that his weakened heart would be continuously exposed to the pressures of life in India.

Knowing Donna was safe and our father in good hands, our mother took Vanessa and me to a food stall to feed us for the first time that day. She bought us each a *naan* bread and small portion of curry. She limited herself to a cup of tea, explaining she didn't feel like eating, which I didn't believe. Sitting in the public restaurant—filthy as we were—she told us we had a ways to travel to visit someone she called Aunt Evans who was letting us stay with her.

"Who is she?" I asked. My mother knelt down beside me. "She's a lady I know, Jillu," she replied, brushing the worst of the dirt from my face. I nodded. I had no doubt that if my mother knew she'd help us, she had to be nice. I couldn't have been more wrong.

5 | Under the Stairs

The naan and curry injected Vanessa and me with a boost to keep going until we reached the Evans' home. We arrived at about 8 p.m., wrapping up an eighteen-hour excursion. We were exhausted and longed to place our heads on a pillow and sleep.

We turned a corner into a narrow lane where a multitude of cheap food shops sold naan bread, wraps, curries, and tea. Mixed among the shops were dilapidated and rundown buildings where people eked out an existence. My mother stopped by the side of open concrete stairs that ran up the outside of a building, leading to a doorway. She told us to wait there while she went to talk to Mrs. Evans and her sister, both of British ancestry.

"Come girls, we have a place to sleep," said my mother on her return. She was behind me. I'd not seen her come back down the stairs.

"Where, Mummy?" I asked expectantly.

"It's not much, Jillu, but Aunt Evans has been very kind to let us stay there."

Before Dum Dum we'd slept on floors and verandas and in disgusting rooms. This, however, was much worse. We entered the

building, and to the right of the door was what I could only describe as a concrete narrow passage where someone could stand. On the wall was this large dilapidated wooden box that had over a dozen electric meters in it. We were about to bed down outside within a common passageway.

We survived the first night unscathed. But on the second we suffered torrential rain with no shelter. We somehow got through that night as well. Had we hit rock bottom? Living in a public passage had the unique benefit of being in the way of residents passing over us making their way in and out of the building. We were to them, to put it mildly, an annoyance. This couldn't last. But we had nowhere else to go. Mum reached out again to Aunt Evans. She said we could live under the concrete stairs (her stairs). No one would ask us to move out or get rude to us there. It wasn't what I'd call an upgrade. It was more exposed than near the meter box and essentially a drain.

Our first home under the stairs

The area we now called home was no bigger than a narrow two-seat dining table. It was full of water from holes in the ground and a nearby well pump. Slime and mildew draped the single back wall and the underside of the stairs and vermin crawled constantly over the entire space. Someone had lived there at one time, and the ground beneath the stairs had in various spots eroded and seeped with stinking damp.

But, in her resolute way, our mother soothed and lifted our spirits with beaming smiles and boundless energy.

"Look, little ones," she said, bending down as usual to our level, "we have to stay here until Daddy gets well again. We have to be strong for him and then we'll find somewhere else where we can be together."

Under the stairs

"But Donna's not sick," said Vanessa. "I want Donna back."

"Well now, there's not enough room for Donna here is there?" said our mother, "so she's got to stay somewhere else. The bad people who wanted us to leave Dum Dum can't find us if we are here, and Donna is safe too."

"Will Donna come back to us when Daddy gets well?" I asked.

"I don't see why not, but let's wait and see, shall we Jillu?" she replied. I nodded. I had learned by that point to do what our parents said. We had no alternative but to go with the flow, no matter what it might be. We might complain but we never openly disobeyed.

In a city full of desperate people, our neighborhood was where the lowest class people—the poorest of the poor—could find a simple meal for one or two *rupees* (a rupee is about one penny or two cents). It was an extremely impoverished area riddled with crime and many disgusting things, not least rats the size of cats. The side of Aunt Evans' and other buildings served as neighborhood toilets, which we'd discovered the first night of our arrival.

Vanessa and I craved a return to Dum Dum. To keep us realistic, our mother set out to make improvements, challenging us to find plastic sheeting to lay on the ground for sleep. We added old bedding

two women begrudgingly gave us. My mother had us look at our living arrangements as a favor, something to appreciate. We had nowhere else to go. It was a roof over our heads and a shelter from heat and rain. My mother reminded us often that others were worse off. Countless others around us didn't even have a place like we had under the stairs.

During this time, the two "ladies" upstairs—I find it difficult to address them as such—imperiously ruled us and made us do their bidding. They shouted at us repeatedly, requiring us to make their beds and clean the floors of the two tiny rooms they had upstairs and downstairs while our mother was away searching for a few rupees to round up some food. They'd send us to a nearby shop to buy tea or a local grocery store for whatever they needed. It seemed some days we were running errands from morning to night.

Our mother hated leaving us during the day, but better that, she felt, than dragging us all over the city. Sometimes she'd find a job for a few hours, cleaning perhaps, but often she'd go to the Anglo-Indian Association, which maintained a small office for Anglo-Indians in desperate need. She'd stand outside for handouts. Sometimes the association gave her a list of people who hadn't paid subscriptions to collect. She'd earn five or ten rupees for her efforts.

Alternatively, she'd go to the Sisters of Charity for handouts of food, perhaps some milk and a couple of biscuits. She scoured the neighborhood, visiting other friends, seeking whatever little they could give for her to bring to us. She did whatever she could and often went hungry, so Vanessa and I didn't.

We lived in public, exposed to whoever passed by en route to food shops or fetch water from the pump a few feet away from our bedding. That pump served as the sole water supply for hundreds of families and people who washed their clothes, spat, and bathed. Our under-the-stairs sanctuary seemed never dry.

Our location did allow us to get to know numerous locals. Frequently, when our mother couldn't bring back anything, the

guard from the local cinema brought us sweets or made his children share their lunch with us. It didn't take Vanessa and me long to know with whom we should end up at lunchtime. We became the best of friends while we lived there.

There were local traders, aware of families in greatest need, who kindly helped out when they could. One sometimes gave us stale, soiled, or misshapen goods such as eggs, bread, sweets, and candles for free. Other families or friends shared what little they had. The neighborhood kindness would help define me.

A few local food shops catered to the extremely poor, offering impoverished people an inexpensive meal. The places were tiny and the cooking often occurred over large coal fires, with large, flat woks used to fry meat. Always hungry, Vanessa and I found it difficult to resist the urge to stand in front of the man who worked nearest to the stairs, staring ravenously at the food he prepared. We had a routine. He would shoo us away as if we were lepers. We'd step back one or two paces and then shuffle forward. Frequently, he'd half-heartedly flick hot oil at us from the spoon he was using to stir-fry the meat. We'd laugh and stand firm in purpose, aware that, surrounded as he was with vessels and food, he couldn't chase us. He'd eventually get tired of our persisted presence and would place some meat inside a small roti or naan and push one each into our hands. The food came with the warning that if we came back, we'd be sorry. We'd always come back. He had a soft spot in his heart. He'd never fail to say "Salam" to my mum. He knew we'd fallen on hard times and were way worse off than he was, and he respected my mother.

Despite the kindness and generosity, we experienced, our living conditions exposed us to awful behavior. One day, for example, as we waited for friends, a man rudely pushed past us to urinate between two buildings. As he relieved himself, he leered at us over his shoulder, and when he finished, turned to face us, exposing himself before walking off.

"I don't want to stay here," said Vanessa, tugging on my dress. "My feet hurt, and I want to go back to Dum Dum."

I looked at my little sister, tears trickling down her cheeks. I felt as she did. I looked down at my bruised and bloodied feet. They hurt too. I turned to her, drew her close, and hugged her.

Local men constantly harassed us. They made lewd comments, called us lurid names, and, worse, tried to touch or abuse us. Even as little as we were, many tried to make us sit on their laps and fondle us. I remember one man touching my chest and then giving me a sweet. While it confused me, I knew it was utterly horrible.

My mother, though, had it far worse.

Cooking, cleaning, and running errands, she worked for Aunt Evans and her sister in return for the place under the stairs. They gave her no money and both beat my mother frequently in front of us. We tried to intervene but learned quickly that our pleas worsened the situation.

The beatings were supposedly for not performing tasks as directed, as they arbitrarily contrived rules as they went along. Impossible to please by their own devious design, they used any pretext to find error in whatever my mother did to satisfy their malicious sadism. When they found nothing wrong, they fabricated something to prompt a beating and threatened to toss us out if she didn't obey. My mother endured the violence because we had no better option.

Looking back, I have immense respect and gratitude for our mother's strength and the love she had for all of us. Despite what we'd been through in our young lives—including Dum Dum and losing our siblings and our home—she did her best to ensure Vanessa and I were relatively happy living under the stairs. As children, we adapted and took it in stride. We were skin and bone, but we smiled and played and cried like other kids and didn't obsess about what we lacked.

My mother continued to use storytelling to buoy our spirits. She made us say our prayers and kneel beneath the moonlight and recite

"Gentle Jesus." We counted stars and huddled together to fall asleep. When we awoke, her long day of work had well started and she'd have something lovely waiting for us, usually a couple of *halwa-puris* (semolina pudding and flatbread)—and a huge smile—to start our day.

Whenever she brought us food, she'd insist that only Vanessa and I eat. At first, we'd hold back, saying, "But Mummy, what about you?" The answer was always the same. I can still see her standing there, offering the food with one hand and waving away our concern for her with the other, saying something like, "Oh, my friend just fed me and I'm just bursting with food! I can't eat another morsel I'm so full!"

The truth, of course, was that she hadn't had a hearty meal, if she'd eaten anything at all. Sometimes she went days without eating. Sometimes, she'd become so weak she would have to stop and rest when covering a short distance or working briefly. She'd close her eyes, steady herself, and keep going about her daily chores.

The extreme hunger, the stress of providing for two small children, the constant beatings, and demanding physical work had taken a toll. Her health began to deteriorate.

She didn't have a real pair of shoes, only two pieces of scrounged leather, wrapped around her feet and held together with string. Yet, she'd set out every morning, leaving us to play for the day with the cinema guard's children until she returned, tired and often empty-handed. The amazing thing was, I don't recall her ever complaining, not once. We never saw anything negative from her, only love, kindness, and a determination to do what it took to save her children. Worse, my father's recovery was taking longer than expected, leaving Mum with the single parenting responsibility for more than she could mentally and physically manage. She bravely soldiered on, day after day.

Under the steps was no place for anyone to live and not surprisingly, Vanessa's and my health also started to deteriorate. The fetid ditch of stagnant run-off water, which stretched across the width in front of

our living space, bred disease, and gave off the foulest of odors. We were frequently ill from near-starvation and malnourishment, and where we slept, roaches and vermin came out of muddy holes in the perpetually damp flooring. Without proper clothes to wear, the squalor increasingly affected our health. We contracted dysentery.

Our mother decided it had to end. She had to find a place with a roof for us. She arranged for us to stay with a woman named Mrs. Green—"a good friend" as she put it—who had agreed to take good care of us. Things began to look up. Little did we know.

6 | Mrs. Green

In the West, I have met women who suffered unthinkable grief from the loss of children. Most had the good fortune of emotional support and help to guide them through the challenge of coming to grips with one of life's harshest realities. My heart goes out to them.

I struggle to erase the recurring visions of my mother's broken heart as she dealt with the grief of the death of one child after another, four in all. Apart from having my dear father, she bore it all virtually alone. How was that possible?

It astounded me that she found the strength to keep going, overcoming one devastating, soul-wrenching blow after another to her psyche, in a country with exceedingly scarce resources and no welfare. Her extraordinary ability to stay the course makes me, by comparison, feel blessed to have only what came my way, and how lucky I was not to face anything remotely comparable. Kindness comes in many forms, and the memory of my mother is a bouquet of her rare gifts, indomitable will, unflagging determination, and unselfish devotion to others.

Not everyone rises to that level.

Take, for example, Mrs. Green, the woman who took Vanessa and me in to rescue us from a life under the stairs. When my mother approached Mrs. Green, she was broken and demonstrably concerned for our health, safety, and development. She beseeched—no begged—Mrs. Green to care for us. Mrs. Green owned a proper house and said she was more than happy to look after and educate us. My mother jumped at the chance. It was a Godsend moment.

We counted our chickens too early.

An eccentric woman who resembled an old witch with foul breath, Mrs. Green constantly beat us. She had a knack for contriving excuses to inflict abuse. Within days, my sister and I began to huddle in corners, living in fear of what she'd do next. There were hand slaps, pokes with sharp sticks, spoons, and brooms, and she used a long mallaca cane to strike us. Her cruelty terrorized us, and the more terrified we were, the more inspired she became to load up the punishment. Our fear was her mode of "education," like a pointer in a classroom. She delivered her teachings from the ends of physical weapons. She was downright mean and cruel.

I was only seven years old at the time. I was innately nervous and shy. The combination of family deaths, illness, and severe poverty, and the worry I carried for my father, still recovering, and my mother living under the stairs, stretched me to emotional limits. The more violent Mrs. Green became, the more withdrawn I became. It morphed into a cycle. As bullies do, Mrs. Green seized upon my palpable insecurity and unsteadiness to make me her favorite target.

Her education "lessons" paralyzed me with fear and rendered me speechless. I constantly stood motionless, waiting for the next onslaught. She'd ask me a question and I would be too intimidated and frightened to think of the answer. A non-response earned more slaps and beatings from our guardian. I never raised an arm or put up any other form of self-defense.

Vanessa unwittingly exacerbated the problem. She was a natural charmer and had a mischievous and endearing glimmer in her eyes. People gravitated to her and she tended to become everyone's favorite. The same followed with Mrs. Green. Vanessa would hide my pencil, draw on my book, or do some other forbidden act, which inevitably enflamed the ire of Mrs. Green, who assumed I was the culprit. I never gave Vanessa up. I owned the misdeed for her and took the punishment.

I was normal in appearance, but Mrs. Green insisted my eyes were out of kilter, one peering horizontally, the other vertically. She insisted that was why I was slow and unable to grasp things. She told my mother I'd never be good at anything. There was nothing wrong with me, except that I cowered in fear and was traumatized.

One day, as part of daily abuse, she made me stand and face the wall in a dark and damp corner

Vanessa and me in our school uniforms

crawling with cockroaches. I screamed, disclosing how petrified I was of cockroaches, especially larger ones. When Mrs. Green learned of my phobia, she cackled in a way that rivaled the chilling voice of the wicked witch in the Wizard of Oz. And, worse, it inspired her to design her evilest atrocity.

Holding me by my ear so I could only stand on tiptoes, she took me to the back of the house and the location of her Indian-style toilet.

The space was half the size of a telephone booth, filthy, and cramped, teeming with a rancid odor beyond description. Vanessa and I only used that toilet when we had no other choice, going together, and leaving the door open while one went and the other waited outside. It was several levels beyond gross.

"Just look in there," she croaked, pointing a crooked finger into that obnoxious chamber of misery. "It's so smelly, but wait ... what's that moving about on the walls?"

I was too petrified to speak. I squirmed to get away. She gripped and pulled my ear tighter and kicked me on the ankle.

"Oh, dearie me, is that hundreds of those huge, flying cockroaches? They don't like the light," she bent down to whisper in my other ear, "They love it when it's dark."

Introduction made, she pushed me inside and, trying not to stick a foot into the hole in the toilet, I stumbled against the wall, my hands brushing up against hordes of cockroaches. As they started flying around me, she turned off the light and locked me in the toilet.

I tried to get as small as I could, melding into darkness, with those awful creatures crawling on my legs and arms. I covered my face with hands and screamed, as they bombarded and got into my ears. Within moments, I felt wee trickling down my leg. I wanted to be sick. I wanted to die. That first night, I spent at least an hour there.

Each day thereafter I had panic attacks anticipating a return to the torture chamber, as it became a ritual. Mrs. Green gave me no relief. She said the roach-infested toilet was where I belonged, what I deserved because of who I was. Every evening she'd force me towards the toilet, open the door, show me the cockroaches, and push me inside. I could take beatings. But I preferred death to being locked inside there. I never emerged from that torture chamber without having wet myself. I developed an association between darkness and being locked in that space. If it went dark during the day during the monsoon season, I'd hyperventilate.

Vanessa sometimes huddled outside the toilet and talked to me. She'd say "Jillu, stand still, if you stand still, they will not fly." But before long, she'd get dragged away by her ear, and in the silence that followed, I could hear only the pounding of my heart. I could not move a muscle for fear of sending the cockroaches flying again once they'd settled after darkness. I could feel them on my skin and in my hair but could do

The toilet that Mrs. Green used to lock me in

nothing about it. I had to wait until she relented to free me. I was in there for at least an hour each night.

When my mother paid a visit, Mrs. Green made sure we didn't say a word. It took a lot to frighten Vanessa, even from an early age, but she kept quiet for fear she'd earn a severe punishment. I assumed Mum knew something wasn't right because I now spoke with a stutter and my body trembled continuously. But what could she do? Mrs. Green gave us a roof over our heads, food, and an education. Mummy didn't know about the abuse and probably thought, all things considered, it was the best place for us until our father recovered and returned.

It was unbearable watching my mother leave after an all-too-short and infrequent visit. As soon as she left, I'd brace for more sessions in the toilet. I often had high temperatures. I cried myself to sleep. I prayed the next day would never come.

Then Mrs. Green started to act differently. She seemed to be aging and disinterested in us, as if she preferred us gone. When not

cruel, she acted almost normal. We no longer were worth the bother. She didn't have the energy for us.

By this time as well, our mother started to sense something was terribly wrong. I am sure she took notice during visits of our pain and unhappiness. But the clincher came during a visit when, while we were standing there, I wet myself. My mother knew the time had come to take us away from there, even though it meant living under the stairs. By that time I must have spent the nights of three months in that toilet as my punishment for a perceived misstep.

Crazy as it sounds, returning to life under the stairs was bliss for Vanessa and me. I felt enormous relief from the absence of daily fright, beatings, and life in that torture chamber. It is hard to describe. Perhaps it is akin to what someone feels walking out of prison after a long incarceration, even awaiting a life of struggle on the outside. I wouldn't have swapped it for the best toy in the world. Vanessa and I laughed and cried together the day Mummy told us to pack our things. I was so happy I developed a high temperature from sheer excitement.

The return journey was long, and ordinarily, as malnourished as I was, I'd have struggled to make the trek. But I skipped the entire way, I was so filled with joy. Vanessa and I teased each other the entire way back, giggling at the silliest and unfunny things. The excitement I felt was unprecedented and immeasurable.

The dark, cold, wet, and dismal place under the stairs was paradise awaiting.

Delighted to be with our mother again, we sat and played as she gazed fondly at us, glad to see us so happy. She didn't know the details—we kept them from her—but she knew we had suffered. She did the best she could to make it up to us. She smiled and laughed when we made up songs about Mrs. Green, but as was her way, she never failed to caution us. "No matter what, we need to be grateful to Mrs. Green for having fed and kept you; let's not forget that." I had no clue at the time how foreshadowing those words were.

7 | History Lesson

I would, over time, understand and appreciate why the family had to separate, why Donna got sent away to live with different people and my father remained hospitalized for so long. My father's absence was especially painful. I was too young to realize it at the time, but his absence induced in me separation anxiety. I worried more. My senses became duller. I often felt anxious and disconnected.

Following our frantic escape from Dum Dum, we didn't see Daddy for weeks on end. Mummy had her hands full, and then some, working and trying to please two women bullies. She lacked the luxury of spare time to do anything other than focus on what the reduced family needed. Visiting the hospital was not an option.

While Mum characteristically repressed what she felt from not having Daddy by her side, his absence had to gnaw at her each day. Despite the brave face she put on for us, I had to believe she shed many a tear privately. The challenges we faced made it impossible for her not to feel the enormous weight of single parenting in our circumstances.

I don't think a woman could be more beaten down than she was in those days. She never overcame the loss of babies Carol and

Mini—was that even humanly possible?—before she had to face the deaths of twins Kimberly and Alan. She then barreled through the upheaval of losing our home, the trauma of protecting Donna from evil men, and the internal torment of keeping Vanessa and me in such terrible conditions. To not have her husband by her side to help navigate it all had to drain her spirit.

How does someone manage that? Where do you go to find hope in repeated distress, emotional pain, and darkness? Looking back, how she rose to the occasion was testament not only to her extraordinary character but to what the mind and spirit are capable of achieving. It was an uncommon display of the power of human resilience, a trait that would become central in my life outlook.

For our part, Vanessa and I didn't suffer in silence. We made clear how much we missed Daddy and relentlessly nagged Mummy for a hospital visit. Eventually, we got a response.

"If you're good I'll take you to see your father, but don't get upset when you see him, and don't worry him with what you hear or see here. Do that and I won't take you to see him again."

Our vigorous nods did the trick. We were more than happy to conspire to protect our father from disturbing information. We were thrilled as it was to know we'd soon see Daddy. A deal of silence was a no-brainer.

And so the visits began. Of course, as soon as we saw him, Vanessa and I wanted to throw open the floodgates and tell him everything. We had a reservoir of stories and angst roaring inside to share. There was so much for him to know. But sworn to secrecy, we kept our word.

My father didn't make it easy. To be expected, at least initially, he peppered us with questions about how Mum was managing, what she had to do to make things work for the family, whether our temporary caretakers treated us well, and on and on. Vanessa and I exchanged discrete whispers about whether to tell all, but in the end, we stayed

the course. We ducked our father's questions with pithy half-truths. All was well. Not to worry.

He knew better of course. He knew we kept much from him and our life was beyond difficult and at times downright intolerable. He knew because he knew the world in which we lived. Many years later, he told me he was well aware that things were awfully hard for our mother. "But she's a very strong woman," he said with profoundly sad eyes, "and I know she'd never let you tell me the truth. I knew things were not good and I felt utterly helpless to do something about it."

Keeping quiet had another benefit: It placed us in a temporary make-believe world, as if the past had disappeared or been suspended. It allowed our visits to morph into joyous excursions away from the harsh realities we faced outside hospital doors. It was an illusion that wouldn't last of course, but it was welcome. We smiled a lot during hospital visits.

The first visit was a high point. We learned straight off that my father's sight had returned as the doctor had predicted. It was a huge relief, and we could see immediately he was in much better spirits. He'd also connected with his fellow patients, most of whom were, like him, ex-servicemen, suffering from one ailment or another. They kept each other engaged, proud, and cheery. Our father made friends with them all. He had two favorites who told us they'd take care of him for us.

I have fond memories of the hospital visits. Knowing we were coming, Dad had his last meal of the day waiting for us. First thing, Vanessa and I would dive bomb onto the food like there was no tomorrow.

The other patients were happy to see us as well. We'd run all about and greet them as "Uncle." They gave us sweets and biscuits. We sat on their knees while they told us stories.

While we frolicked about, my mother always took the opportunity to bend the ears of medical staff with instructions about what my

father needed. "Now listen," she would begin, "he tends to gasp a lot when there is a cardiac arrest coming on. He tends not to ask for help; he is a quiet and proud man who doesn't share his problems and won't tell you if he is feeling bad."

The visits also gave me cherished private time with my father and a chance to display the inquisitive mind he always told me I had. Vanessa by nature gravitated to the attention of the uncles, while I, more reserved, liked to sit with my father, comb his hair, fluff his pillows, and engage in conversation. One time he treated me to a history lesson. I had mentioned I wanted to learn more about why we differed from most people around us. He smiled and patted the bed. I took the cue and took up a place next to him.

"That's an interesting question, Jillu," he began, "because while Dum Dum offered us so much hope—a proper future with security and stability—it is because we were different that we had to escape."

"But we're all people, Daddy. We all have heads and arms and legs and hearts."

"But there are differences aren't there?" He asked. He paused, waiting for my reply.

"Well … I guess it's because we look different, our skin is much lighter, and we speak a different language, or is it because we dress differently?"

He nodded his head in encouragement and held forth.

"While we were born in India, we have what's called British and Scottish ancestry. Your grandparents came from England and the name that many know us by is Anglo-Indian. But, in our family, we refer to ourselves as just a family, we love India but our blood is British and Scottish, but deep down, we are all still people with the ability to love or hate, to pick people up or drag them down, to bring joy to others or not, and so on.

"One day, you will go to England and discover that while we may look like the people there, your heart, your soul, and your mind all

belong here. It's how I felt when my sister was returning to the UK. It's a battle that many people all over the world face, especially those who emigrate—move to another country—the human brain is somewhat set by the age of twenty-one, and after that, there is little you can do to change the way you feel. People move for prosperity—a better life—to be happier and to give their children a better chance in life but most often, they are unfulfilled because it's as though someone has taken a cutting of their tree to another land and planted it there but the root remains where they were born and where they grew up.

"However, other people don't always understand these things and so they rebel and abuse and hurt others because little knowledge is a dangerous thing. It is so hard for people to understand these things, and so many like us and others all over the world suffer far too much at the hands of the ignorant.

"You know from the people who have helped us like Mrs. Brown, that there are others like us in the center of Calcutta, but there aren't that many left, because most of the British people left when India got her …"

He smiled at me, waiting for me to fill in the blank. We'd talked about this in Dum Dum.

"Inde … inde … independence!" I said happily. He clapped softly and smiled.

"And the year?"

"1947!"

"Very good!"

My father had previously taught us that in 1935, the Indian government passed a law that defined Anglo-Indian as a person whose male lineage was European but who was a native of India, and that when India gained independence from Britain in 1947, many Anglo-Indians left the country. Most emigrated to English-speaking British Commonwealth countries such as the UK, Canada, and Australia. Some two to three thousand Anglo-Indians couldn't afford

to emigrate an entire family, which included my parents. For them, survival became the primary life goal. The lucky ones had secure jobs or skills they could peddle into work.

In 1962, my father met my mother. He was in the unfortunate circumstance of separating from his first wife and their children. My mother's life was no different during that period. Her first husband had abandoned her and their two small children to go to the UK. She had nothing and nowhere to go. All of her siblings were in the UK already and she would never see them again. When my parents met and began their relationship of twenty-seven years, both were destitute, battling to keep body and soul together, always finding themselves at the back of the job-seeking queue with fellow Anglo-Indians.

Outcasts or non-castes—call us whatever you like—we were the product of two incompatible and canceling cultures, either visible and deemed non-existent or existent but invisible.

To my young mind, it was all very confusing. What difference did it make that we had fairer skin, spoke English with a distinct accent, dressed differently, and were not Muslim or Hindu but Christian?

"But why doesn't everyone else like us? We get called all sorts of names."

"I'm afraid to say that's mostly ignorance, Jillu. To many local people, although not all, we are associated with people who were disliked in the past, ruled their country, hurt many of their people, and were not wanted. We are cursed with the stain of history."

That was as much as I could get my young head around at that time, that the situation made us outcasts or non-castes. For some local people, our heritage, race, religion, and ways of living imprinted a disapproving label on our foreheads.

Beyond fairer skin, the other distinctive trait is the accent of our mother tongue. It may be surprising, but it was more the accent that made us different. It makes us sound Indian, and a foreigner

speaking to us on the telephone probably couldn't tell we were mostly fair-skinned, blond, English people. Not so for the locals. To them, we sounded distinctly different and for some reason, it alienated people. Those distinguishing linguistic variations, in many respects, perversely alienated us more than the fact that in their country, we did not speak in Hindi, Bengali, or other Indian languages.

With our social consciousness and identities mostly being ignored, if not wholly suppressed, my siblings and I were vanishing remnants of a bygone era. Much has been written about the caste system in India, but there was no place in their hierarchy of society for us, not even at the bottom. Essentially, we were ghosts and many wished for us to vanish. To be Anglo-Indian might sound exotic, but it's far from a mark of positive distinction.

I've always thought that had we been born in the West, or in many other different countries, those like me could have established deeper foundations from which to build a successful life. People say adversity builds character, making a person stronger in the long run. But it's not so easy when the only reality you have is adversity.

The term my father first used—Anglo-Indian—is much maligned and abused. It began in reference to the children of British soldiers or traders who had the "good fortune"—a difficult concept for those like me to grasp—of growing up in India because their parents moved there. There are many famous examples from days past, such as Rudyard Kipling or Jim Corbett, but by 1947 when the British government had officially withdrawn, most Anglo-Indians had left in search of greener pastures.

By that time, the erstwhile Eurasians—those who had a British father and a local mother—had also appropriated the term. The locals viewed them as even poorer cousins to us. But practices and perceptions change, and what grew out of this was that anyone in India with a slightly Christian-sounding name thought it would be beneficial to be associated with Britain. They proudly referred to

themselves as Anglo-Indian, an idea even adopted by some foreign-born people who had no connections whatsoever.

But most history books do not recount such things amid the turmoil of Indian Independence and the mass exodus of most of the Anglo-Indians that followed. But authors of history books are selective, and they certainly viewed Eurasians as a minority of no importance.

There were, however, an unfortunate few and genuine Anglo-Indian families who either chose to remain in India after 1947 or, more often, were forced to do so due to health issues or, more likely, financial constraints. My parents qualified as one such unfortunate couple; both born in India, they never had the resources to leave. They were destined to be lost among the teeming millions toiling in the streets of Calcutta.

8 | Kidderpore

A year passed before my father's health improved to where he could come home. Seeing him up and about brought palpable joy to all of us. I don't think any of us felt the true impact of missing him so much as when he returned. We cherished watching him get back to his vigorous self, doing all the little things he did to make life a little bit happier for the family, flashing us back to the Dum Dum days. We had all been through a lot, but his return signaled better times ahead as a family. Slim reeds of hope slipped into the everyday creases of our lives.

Donna remained with friends in central Calcutta, although we saw her as often as we could. Vanessa and I came to accept our separation from her. What we didn't know was that Donna's experiences were as hard as ours, or maybe even worse, as she was not with people who loved or cared for her. She lived with a woman who treated her as a source of income. She began as the family servant, responsible for menial domestic tasks. But despite being bullied and mistreated, she grew stronger and stood up for herself. She knew we were destitute. She fought hard to survive and did what she could to help us, and as God is my judge, she did.

The weight of Donna's tribulations took a heavy toll, shaping her outlook and character. She became formidable and incorrigible and sometimes downright impossible. Many avoided, hated, or feared her. She had overcome serious atrocities, better left unsaid. She managed to get strong, but at a price. She developed survival tools most of us are spared. I know now how and why this sweet, beautiful, blue-eyed, blond-haired girl could turn vicious, hateful, or violent at the drop of a hat. She also has a heart of gold. She helped save our lives. She did the best she could with the resources she had. I owe her and I will never forget that.

My father found a job in the administrative department of MRF, a tyre manufacturer. The pay was markedly meager, which undercut efforts to find living accommodations. For the time being, we jammed into a local hotel, near the stairs under which we previously lived, known as Biru's Lodge. It was a temporary solution. We couldn't afford to stay long at the hotel, because of the long-term costs, and it was becoming nigh on impossible to find a place to rent because of required deposits and guarantees.

I might point out that calling Biru Lodge a hotel was generous. It was a damp and decaying place that provided minimal shelter for a few rupees. The rooms were small and cramped. The ceiling leaked and the walls were cracked. Our room had a single filthy window the size of what you'd find in a prison cell. There was a single pull-down bed, a light bulb, and a wooden stool for a table. Vanessa and I slept on the floor.

One early evening, my father came home from work looking out of sorts. He began coughing blood. My mother gave him water and made him lie down while I sprinted to the pharmacy for tablets and to call Dr. Sinha. Later that evening, the doctor confirmed what we

suspected, that he had suffered a minor cardiac arrest. The doctor kindly didn't charge us for his time or the medications.

A few days after the latest scare, Mr. Nazareth passed away. His death felt like the entire world had cascaded upon us. That beautiful man was our guardian angel, our go-to for help and counsel. He never failed to be there for us in times of need, and now we'd lost him too. His death devastated the family.

Within a few weeks, my father got better, took an advance from work—a loan that accrued interest—and rented us something with a roof in Kidderpore, a severely impoverished area southwest of Calcutta. The Kidderpore dwelling was close to where my siblings attended boarding school. Otherwise, little commended it.

We had a single ten-by-six-feet room into which, in addition to our scrawny bodies, we jammed one bed, a metal chair, two small tables, and a small metal trunk. We placed each precious item along walls with their top to bottom damp layer of mold over old green paint. My parents used the bed and my sister and I again slept on the floor.

The inside of our little room in Kidderpore

The floor rippled with cracks from wall to wall, home to all manner of insects and rats, which tended to visit at night. My mother tried to seal the crevices with mud and other materials, but the cracks kept reappearing. Over time we managed to reduce the infestation, but the little unwelcome visitors never went away entirely, no matter how hard we tried. We didn't have a fridge and stored food under the table, protected by an old sheet slipped under the table legs. It was not uncommon to lift the sheet to see rats lounging around from the prior night or an entire plate of food covered in cockroaches.

The place had what served as a "veranda" off the entrance in a narrow passageway, a ten-by-four-feet concrete space where we kept three buckets of water, a replacement kerosene stove someone had given us, and a small coal-burning mud oven. Since we were on the ground floor, we kept a few bricks outside to prevent sewage water collecting in a ten-inch-wide and six-inch-deep drain, which hundreds of families used, from seeping onto the veranda and into the room. We succeeded as often as we didn't.

Adjacent to the passageway entrance stood three public bathrooms, which over three thousand people shared. Never cleaned, and infested with cockroaches, lizards, and rats, they had no flushing capacity. The stench was indescribable and constant.

Further to the left was a cleared area with a tube well that all the people in the adjoining buildings used for rubbish. Crawling with rats, dozens of other pests, and thousands of flies, it was where people tossed daily waste and used as a public toilet. Local people fed pigs there too and sold the meat to families who lived nearby. It was disgusting.

A lady visited twice a week to clean the drain. She picked up everything she could with either an empty opened tin can or her bare hands, putting all the detritus in a bucket. She then threw the contents into a huge dustbin across the road. You could smell it miles away.

The Kidderpore rent was sixty rupees per month which later increased to 100 rupees—approximately £1. While seemingly modest, we struggled to stay current, which in turn led to a barrage of incessant landlord threats to boot us out of the place. Our financial problems were mainly due to the work advance of 500 rupees my father received to rent the place initially, which eventually put a major crimp on cash flow. It wasn't until I started working that we were able to chip away at the debt.

Our family room-home was one of thousands in the higgledy-piggledy slums that comprised the Kidderpore section of Calcutta. Our street lacked a road name and people used visual aids to find us. And yet, the four walls around us were our sanctuary—the first stable home I'd known. With our own front door and neighbors who looked out for us, our tiny room was a palace compared to our previous place, a dank stairwell next to a drain.

Despite the conditions, living in one place as a family unit brought happiness and stability into our lives. Believe it or not, we were thrilled to be there. It was our home. My father was regaining his health. My mother was not being beaten. And Vanessa and I didn't live in fear. And, above all, the four of us were together. The family felt emboldened to face whatever hardships might come our way and hopeful we'd settle down to a normal life.

We enjoyed rituals again. My father made tea each morning before leaving for work. He became the primary earner in the family again and come hail, rain, storm, or sickness, he went to work while our mother looked after us. Mum taught English to young children from the area, and while it did not earn her much, it allowed her to stay home to look after Vanessa and me.

In 1978, we were blessed with a new family member, Neil Terrance. My brother was born in a local free hospital and my mother and he were sent home the same day. By the time he arrived, my mother was exhausted, which meant the rest of us got to care for

the baby and Mum. Neil was malnourished in the early days, but we helped him get stronger each day. I have etched in my mind the heartwarming picture of my mother, sheer joy on her face, her eyes full of love, holding her healthy baby. Life can be beautiful.

During his recuperative stint with the Salvation Army, my father taught himself shorthand, which led to a job as a stenographer with a law firm (L.S. Davar & Company). It was quite the accomplishment. Getting another job at his age was hard enough, but reinventing himself to do so was on a whole new level. The transition from senior military officer to stenographer doubtlessly took courage, but characteristically Dad stepped up to help the family survive.

I should point out that despite the troubles we had, I have a perpetual soft spot for the wonderful people in our local community. I would over time come to believe that for every misfortune or devastation there is a parallel kindness, and that when push comes to shove, kindness triumphs over difficult or seemingly impossible odds. Despite appalling living conditions, limited resources, and getting the short of the stick year-in and year-out, many people we came across had hearts of gold. They consistently showered us with kindness, warmth, and generosity.

A local tea shop owner gave us *samosas*—little wraps filled with savory vegetables and herbs—or whatever else he had made that day in his shop. He would always give us one or two for free, broken ones he couldn't sell. They were treasures to us and we were moved by his bigheartedness. He'd see us coming and flash a quick, broken-toothed grin before he looked around to make sure no one was watching. He didn't want others to see him giving away food. But he liked us because we were fair and different from the other kids, staring at him with mouths agape in front of his huge cooking vessel. Watching him had a lingering influence on us.

He wasn't alone in his kindness. The *dal-puri* (lentils and flatbread) man would give Mum dal-puris & halwa-puris (mainly on weekends). It was a treat. My mum used to pay him a few rupees and bring home the packet of puris for us all. Getting something special to eat was such a happy occasion.

The grocery shop that never asked for payment

We also received vegetables from the local produce woman vendor, bones from a local butcher, and sundries from the grocery vendor we called Modi.

A local barber gave us free haircuts. He'd put a plank of wood across the big wooden armrests of chairs so that we were high enough to look in the mirror to watch his handiwork. We'd complain that he made us look like boys and my mother would shush us, telling us we looked nice and pointing out that the short cut would keep us cool in the summer, be easy to wash with minimal soap, and wouldn't get knotted. And all that for free! So, stop complaining!

These people loved us dearly, watched over us, fed us, and saved our lives. Words fail me to describe the bounds of their selflessness and kindness. They had so little and shared it all.

Their kindness taught me great life lessons about survival, gratitude, humility, generosity, honesty, trust, and sacrifice. It was where my essence got honed.

9 | Away From Home

Shortly after my father joined the law firm as a stenographer, Vanessa and I became age-eligible to attend the nearby boarding school where my siblings studied. We were able to attend tuition-free because we were dependents of an ex-British serviceman. Institutions like those were a haven for Anglo-Indian children. When I was growing up, India provided automatic state-funded education for children and some local government-run schools existed for the poor, but none provided more than the thinnest of rudimentary education.

The British established the boarding schools in Victorian times and modeled them to mirror the UK educational system. Enrollment was not limited to children from families with considerable means. After the British left India, sponsors living abroad became a fertile source of funds to finance the education and boarding of left behind Anglo-Indian children.

I was a beneficiary of that system and its high educational standards. I shall forever be grateful to those who sponsored my siblings and me. But for their selfless benevolence, we'd not be where we are today.

Vanessa would subsequently go on to complete her teacher's training, gaining qualifications that allowed her to teach in the UK.

I will never forget our school principal, Mr. David Cameron, a man of uncommon integrity and honor. His leadership led to countless Anglo-Indian children receiving a top-flight education and enjoying a foundation on which to build a decent life. Many families benefited from his able and compassionate stewardship. Mr. Cameron took a personal interest in Vanessa and me, making sure we were comfortable, loved, and understood. He watched over us from afar, comforted my parents, and left a lasting impact on our hearts and minds.

Our school, St. Thomas' Girls School, and the Anglo-Indian community, had incredible talent. It produced some of the best athletes in the city and even the country, including my sisters and a cousin. Our sports teacher put on spectacular drill displays, as good as the city had ever seen.

Our drama and music teachers were equally ambitious and impactful. The student body boasted more than our share of excellent singers and actors and they participated in the production of quality shows like *My Fair Lady*, *The Wedding Breakfast*, and *Annie*. Most of these talented and creative children were Anglo-Indians, and following their sound education, later found jobs and success around the world and became successful.

I don't mean to crow about my community. Well, I do a little. But if you had witnessed what I did during my time at school and the outstanding talent from both teachers and students, and if you watched the opening ceremonies at the Olympics or attended a theatre in London, you would know the kind of talent our people possessed. In many respects, it was equivalent or better than what I later paid for in London. Yet many of boundless talent achieved nothing of note, all for the want of an opportunity.

Too often, the talent of many of them never spilled beyond the boundaries of the school or the city. Life after school for many

St. Thomas' Girls School where I received my first formal education

meant returning to the bottom rung, defaulting to the same extreme hardship and need to survive as before. The potential for displaying and developing talent often yielded to the necessity of finding meager sources of income for the most essential things in life.

The talent got wrapped and stored as a treasured journal of one's youth. In those days, India did not cultivate natural abilities in sports and often children not academically minded got left behind. Some had extraordinary artistic talent, but they wanted for opportunities, like singers who couldn't sing in the local language. Few got as much as a second glance.

If our community had a place to call its own, if we were seen as people and not thorns in the side most of the time, if we were given equal opportunity and had our skill and talents appreciated like those of others, we'd have put our stamp on mainstream culture. Instead, we were made to feel less from all quarters, and with poverty

holding most of us down, wound up pitted against each other in a community with which, even today, many want to disassociate.

We were, however, taught to do our best and inspire the generations to follow. We were taught to believe in ourselves and not get discouraged by the many challenges we'd continue to face down the line. Music often captured the spirit of our culture, as we learned songs like Abba's *I Had a Dream*, and its poetic expression of hope, belief in angels, and having the courage to push through the darkest realities. The lyrics taught us to see good in everything despite hardships and helped shape our lives for the better.

As young students, Vanessa and I had more modest preoccupations than the fate and historical challenges of Anglo-Indian culture. We worked hard in school to keep up and often struggled to find a place of belonging among a student body that included many with more affluent means and different backgrounds.

Despite the benefits of our education, and a relatively stress-free daily life, we missed our home and parents terribly. I think part was feeling disconnected at school and part was core longing for family. Thankfully, my father's new job made it possible to afford visits home. Even though that meant returning to squalor, seeing our parents and little brother brought us mounds of joy. We still had limited electricity, no proper drinking water, lousy sanitary conditions, little food, many household chores to resume, and terrible encounters with men everywhere we went, but the short reunions were bliss. We could love and hold our parents, work hard in the spirit of a united family, and display how much we missed them.

We had our hands happily full with domestic chores. We enjoyed washing clothes at the tube well, cleaning pots and pans, and looking after the younger ones.

One chore shall never be forgotten.

We had to collect water from a tube well and transport it to our little room, making our way through a tiny passage over a huge

manhole directly in front of the three community toilets. Sewage and vermin filled the manhole to the brim. As we started to ease our way past the manhole, Vanessa stumbled and before I could react, she fell into the manhole.

My heart immediately sank with a surge of panic. I felt as though every drop of blood had drained from my body. I feared the worst. Vanessa was the closest to me in the family. We were born one and half years apart. We grew up together and went to school together and, most of all, endured so many trials and tribulations together. We were bonded in spirit. And right before my eyes, a major part of me, my little sister, may have slipped to her death.

I was a reticent child, a girl of few words, but that day, I screamed as I had never screamed before, and my father bounded out of the house and immediately gauged the situation. Vanessa was hanging onto the edge of the manhole with her tiny little white fingers screaming for help. All we could see was the top of her head and those little frantic fingers.

My father grabbed her hair and pulled. Vanessa emerged, her fair complexion now red as a ripe tomato. Her face was grazed, she was covered with excretions and smelled like nothing on Earth. My mum washed her down as she trembled like a leaf on a windy day. I tried in vain to help, but my incessant sobbing prevented me from doing much.

That episode became fixed in my psyche. I've never freed myself from the trauma of what happened, haunted by the reality that but for a few seconds of adult intervention, we might have lost Vanessa for good. Taking falls in the communal area was not uncommon. We often lost our balance in the area where the community collected their water and washed their clothes and utensils, sometimes while carrying the little ones. It was always slippery and covered in slime, soap, or bathwater, and we sustained a rash of injuries and scrapes and often cried and laughed. It was integral to living where we did.

But this latest event shook me to the core. For several seconds, my heart stopped and my soul disassembled, a sobering reminder of the dangers lurking in the slum and how each day we often walked a fragile line between life and death.

While our visits home flashed a glaring light on the family's continual hardship, no one complained. We didn't care for toys or fancy clothes. Our parents made sure that when we were home, we engaged as a family and enjoyed ourselves together, which sometimes included outings to a local zoo, complete with a picnic basket filled with whatever we could manage to gather. The price of entry was one rupee and, for us kids, it was a dream come true. I'd get so excited about the thought of going to the zoo I sometimes developed a high fever, which occasionally meant canceling the trip. I became instantly unpopular for a few days! My anticipatory anxiety was so great, my parents withheld zoo plans from me until the last minute. That's the kind of anxiety I suffered in those days.

When stuck at home, our father put on a brave face and tried to make us as happy as he could. He'd buy us an occasional treat, like a small cake, tease and tickle us, and make up songs about our matrons at school. The more fun we had at home, the more Vanessa and I dreaded returning to school. We hated being away from family, especially not seeing our baby brother. We also worried about how they might carry on. We were old enough to understand the extent to which our parents suffered from our living status and financial difficulties.

The time to go back to school meant a rash of tears, entreaties, and promises to do whatever my mother asked to stay another day or two. We wanted to be with the family and to help in any way we could. And the truth is, I for one feared letting go of loved ones in case I never saw them again.

I also feared what awaited us at school. We often were asked to bring working materials to school, like thread for a needlework class, or ink, or polish, or even toothpaste, which we couldn't afford. It was a huge embarrassment. Occasionally we got reprimanded, although, for the most part, the school understood the problem we had and let us off the hook, often finding a way to give us what we needed. The worst was humiliation from feeling inferior.

One time, my mother addressed the problem with ingenuity. I was supposed to bring various food ingredients to school for a competition, but we didn't have the money. Mum found an aubergine and some small tomatoes, which I used to make a doll, with broken earrings and buttons for its face and tomato slices for jacket buttons. To my surprise and delight, I won first prize. It was a valuable lesson about what is needed to succeed.

Sometimes at the boarding school, we had to learn to stand up for ourselves and fight back when someone tried to push us around. It didn't happen often, but when it did, we learned to stand for ourselves. We were honing our street smarts. Our toughness drew respect and we began to connect with other kids and become more popular over time.

Our gracious foreign sponsors continued to help us. We'd received free items from the school, mostly for our lessons, which we later learned were gifts from the sponsors. Occasionally sponsors visited the school and, sometimes, they provided a little extra money for a school fete or a treat. It wasn't much, but since we rarely received any pocket money, it meant a great deal. The school seldom identified the sponsors but did have us write thank-you letters.

Some sponsors visited, roaming about incognito, seeking to adopt school children. I learned later that they from time to time approached our mother (through our school) with offers to take us off her hands. She refused each time, and it infuriated her that the school allowed this practice. As she later recounted, she didn't pull her punches.

"I am grateful for the sponsor's help, but I don't need it if they want my children in return. We might be poor, and we might not have any worldly goods, but I love my children, and no amount of money in the world can part me from them or part them from each other."

Today, when I watch many programs designed to help people find their birth parents, the first question they ask when they find their parents is, "Why did you give me up?" Many point to the specific circumstances at the time or explain they wanted to find a better life for the child. I am proud to say I had a mother who withstood what no woman should go through in her lifetime and yet, she never gave any of us the opportunity to ask the question, "Why did you give us up?"

In 1978, while at school, we confronted a new challenge. It rained continuously for over two weeks, bringing deadly flash floods and the entire city to a standstill and displacing as many as 15 million people. Disease spread rampantly, owing to virtually nonexistent drainage and a lack of proper sanitary arrangements. While we were relatively safe and dry in school, people nearby used upturned beds as boats, food became scarce, and sellers offered basics like bread and vegetables at huge premiums.

The school suspended lessons. The principal offered the school as shelter for local poor people, an offer they took up in droves, crowding into every corridor in the school. We were not allowed out of the dormitories. Despite our relative safety, Vanessa and I became increasingly anxious about our family. There were no phones or means of communication and we were cut off from one another, with no idea of how safe anyone was. Knowing how quickly the drain outside the Kidderpore home could get blocked and fill the room with water, Vanessa and I were worried sick. Throughout the day our eyes were glued to the windows, hoping for a glimpse of our parents and our little brother coming to the school, safe and sound.

Meanwhile, Donna, living and working in central Calcutta, tried to pay a taxi double the amount of money to fetch my parents and my brother or to drop them some food. He refused. Too dangerous, he explained. She finally found another taxi to take her there. They got to the head of the road near the room but the high-water level made it too risky to get further. They had to retreat and head back.

Many weeks later, when the floods subsided, our mother unannounced appeared at the school with our baby brother. On sight, we sobbed our hearts out. My mother was desperately thin from starving and looked utterly depleted of energy and spirit. But when she saw Vanessa and me, she gave us a smile for the ages. At first, we wanted nothing more than to hug them, so relieved we were. We then found a bench to sit on, and she told us what had happened.

The drain outside our room in the slum

The floods rose so high around our one-room home that everything was soon underwater. The torrent was endless because the narrow passage between two huge buildings, less than three feet apart, acted as a funnel, filling much of our ground floor space. In response, our parents tipped the bed on its side and sat on the top edge above rising water.

They had no electricity or food. Everything they owned became saturated. Some items floated around them. The water continued to rise, while

they prayed for it to stop. Not knowing what would happen, they wanted to do what they could to save baby Neil. They planned to leave the baby on the concrete shelf close to the ceiling, hoping the waters would recede and, if they perished, someone eventually could find him.

When she told us how she, my father, and our little brother survived in that room, seated on the edge of the bed for days, Vanessa and I cried inconsolably. It felt worse than the horrible feeling I'd had when we almost lost Vanessa, knowing we could have lost all of them. That they could have drowned in that one room was too much to handle. I felt traumatized listening to the details: envisioning being there, watching it happen in real-time, feeling helpless.

It turns out that most people in Kidderpore were rescued, but my father refused to abandon the family dwelling, never expecting the situation to get so bad. He was a proud man and fell back on his dignity and thought, by hunkering down at home, the family would be spared the degradation and humiliation attendant upon getting shoved inside makeshift shelters for hundreds and hundreds of other flood victims.

My mother believed her prayers saved them, as many nearby were not so fortunate—getting washed away, their bodies later tossed onto piles with hundreds of others who perished. If the rain had persisted much longer, they would have met the most horrifying of deaths, and we might never have known their fate. To this day, I have terribly upsetting nightmares about it, as vivid images of what my mother described fill my mind.

The floods left devastation, illness, and even greater poverty in their wake. It took months to clear things up afterwards. Little of the rehabilitation was handled properly.

When my mother came to see us that day, she brought nothing but her and Neil and an abundance of love and devotion. It mattered not at all that she couldn't bring us treats or had no spare money

for us to buy extra food like virtually every other family did for our classmates. Seeing her and Neil was a blessing. Once they arrived, we wanted for nothing. Each hug fulfilled us beyond description.

The most telling moment came when visiting hours were over and we watched Mum pick up our little brother and trudge away in the mud across the field towards the school gate. It was then that I could see more clearly what she'd become. She moved so slowly, absolutely exhausted, her body but skin and bones. She had tried to make out she was fine and had been invited to a friend's house for dinner. But that was not true. We knew that not only did she have to walk all the way home carrying the baby in her arms, but she was going back to nothing.

Watching her walk out of sight, knowing school would soon feed us dinner, hurt so much. It is impossible to describe that feeling of helplessness; desperately, achingly wanting to be with her, to help her, knowing she had nothing to eat and yet she'd made the arduous and punishing journey on foot to see us. We were worried about my father too, if only because he had pushed himself to go to work to complete that day's work to get paid.

We wanted to return home with her. She wasn't having it. She explained the obvious, we had better shelter and food in school. I have, until this day, never met a woman as strong and astoundingly courageous. It fills me with tremendous pride and gratitude to realize that, above all, this amazing tower of strength was my mother.

10 | Soup in a Bottle

Boarding school provided bare essentials—our own bed and basic board—and kept us away from the dangers we faced as children where we lived. Our poverty, however, continued to play a role at school.

Unlike most fellow students, we rarely received extra food or money to supplement the meager school meals. We sometimes received items like wheat porridge from the US that included worms after a long journey to India. But our hunger overcame the repulsion. We looked on with envy as the day scholars brought in food daily and other boarders bought cakes and biscuits from the canteen. Each day, Vanessa and I hovered near the more fortunate children, waiting to pounce on discarded cake or biscuit wrappers to scrape off remnant crumbs. They tasted so good.

As we familiarized with school routines, we hatched schemes to address our almost incessant hunger. We surveyed dry school drains for a sweet, an apple core or a half-eaten sandwich, anything remotely edible, and if we discovered a prize, we'd jumped into the huge drains, pretending we dropped a pencil. Whenever successful,

we ran to the toilet to wash the morsel under the tap or brush off its dust before sharing our bounty, often one tiny bite each.

When we first enrolled at school, we were tiny, so much so we struggled to reach the dining tables in the refractory. Our food matron kindly brought in a tiny table, like what you'd find in a nursery, and set it up near hers, to which she added two little chairs. Our customized arrangement allowed us to reach our food and learn the basics of eating at a proper dining table.

Boarding school dining hall

Parents could visit the school on Saturdays. When they did, they brought myriad gifts for their children. The other girls received fantastic biscuits and sweets and chocolates and special home-cooked food. Most of the time, when she could, Mum brought us soup in a bottle to supplement what we received from the school. She collected dried and unused bones from a local meat man and boiled them to create the soup. She often brought extra bottles for us to share with fellow students. Our soup in a bottle became a popular item, tasty

and healthy, and other students kept an eye out for Mum's arrival eager to share in what we'd receive.

Our family always lacked money to buy us proper toiletries. It was hard watching other girls each morning brushing their teeth and showering with special soap. The school gave us a cake of soap each month, but it never lasted the month, and often we didn't have toothpaste, prompting us to campaign—toothbrushes in hand—to get some from fellow classmates. A high point of the week occurred whenever a matron gave us a small tube of Colgate toothpaste, which, we later learned, she purchased with her own money.

I struggled to find my place in school. I didn't have an identity. I worked hard, but I was repressed and often withdrew from the others. I lacked social skills and often didn't hold my own with others—a timidity that made me a target for bullies. Vanessa, almost two years younger with more than her share of spunk and mischief, often stood up for me. Whenever someone gave me a hard time, Vanessa intervened, like a brave little warrior, sometimes to the point of fighting. Hunger might get to Vanessa, but fear never ever did. As small as she was, she stood up to bigger and older girls, fearlessly taking them on without batting an eye.

Even though I often longed to come home, where I felt emotionally safe, our parents resisted the visits. They knew we were better off at school than home, a reality that got reaffirmed the times I did go home. There was hardly any electricity. We had little food. We had to look after the younger one. We were surrounded by constant illness. I was always covered in boils, maybe a hundred or more, which I associated with mangoes since I ate the inexpensive fruit all the time during the summer when temperatures tended to hover around 45 to 47 degrees Celsius. To this day, I cannot eat a mango, although it's not at all clear that mangoes were the cause of my illness or instead my body had succumbed to the combination of extreme heat and family stress. Regardless, I didn't let the boils get in my way of helping my parents in any way I could.

So the home visits diminished. I had to make do in a school often filled with hundreds of girls, sleeping alone in a dormitory set up to house many less. I forced myself to integrate into the culture. We played hopscotch and string games, gathered leaves, attended Vocational Bible School, learned acting and singing, took part in handicraft competitions, and met children from other schools and parishes.

Boarding school dormitory

I handled these activities well enough, but I dreaded sports day. I'd get so nervous. I could not do a thing right. Take the long jump. We had three tries, but I would run across the sandpit, unable to jump. Nothing in the world could make me jump, despite the encouragement of the P.E. mistress, a close friend of my mother, who always gave me extra chances. I simply couldn't jump. It was the same with the high jump. I'd run to the pit and dive under the bar. It was embarrassing.

Running was no better. When the gun went off, I stood there and froze. They put me on the relay team! Every girl started the race, but I was still at the start line. They tried putting me as the second or third runner, but it didn't work. I still couldn't run. I had a serious nervous disposition, which manifested itself in odd ways.

Whenever we returned to school after a home visit, we had to stand for inspection. They'd check our heads for lice and take our temperatures. Anyone who didn't pass got sent home and anyone ill to the school infirmary. My frequent high fevers often got me sent home.

My mother determined that I wasn't sick. She knew that my nerves caused my body temperature to spike. It harked back to the ordeals with Mrs. Green. Mum told my matron to admit me to school while she waited. If after an hour, the high temperature persisted, she'd take me home. If not, I could stay in school. It worked. The high temperatures invariably came down.

Even though I was so young at the time, I knew all wasn't right with me. I hated feeling withdrawn and nervous. It made me feel small and isolated. I started writing letters to my father, which helped my spirits. Whenever he replied, I got ecstatic. I'd immediately take the envelope to the toilet, remove the letter, and sit to read in peace and quiet. One time, I expressed anxiety that I'd never accomplish much in school. He responded with a tale from his wartime days in the military and pearls of wisdom from poet Edgar Guest.

> *We walked for days on end with hardly any food or water and sometimes we used to have to carry our friends (other soldiers) on our backs when there weren't enough stretchers. One time after a day and a half and resting very little we got to a camp where there was some food, but the commander in chief would not let us sit down and rest until he addressed us.*

You know what it's like when you get the letters from your wives and your family saying please send more money, more money to pay the rent, more money to pay the school fees, more money to eat, please send more money, and there is nothing more you can do. You send your full salary home. What else do they want you to do? When you face times like that, remember these words …

"When things go wrong, as they sometimes will,
And the road you're trudging seems all uphill,
When the funds are low, and the debts are high,
When you want to smile,
But you have to sigh,
When care is pressing you down a bit,
Rest, if you must, but don't you quit."

The full impact of those words might not have penetrated me at the time, but I got the essential message. I couldn't give up. I couldn't feel sorry for myself. I had to keep on. But there was something else percolating, although I couldn't know it at the time.

It had to do with how I reacted to what my mother went through. Watching Mum struggle so much persistently got me down. I'd stay awake night after night, crying and wanting to run away. I didn't know how I could help, and even if I did, I might have been more of a hindrance, but my heart and mind wanted me out of that school and in that little room to ease some of the pain and assume some of her workload.

One time she let me stay, keeping me from school for almost eight months. I looked after the little ones, fed and nursed them, and handled most of the household chores. I was in my element. Then one morning, Mum woke me up to announce I had to return to school the next day.

The following morning, I woke in a cold sweat. I was anxious about the prospects of a new class and new teacher. I feared how isolated I'd be, with no idea of how to get along. I shuddered to think how everybody would know everything, and I, not a thing. I made another run at my mother. I begged her not to send me back. She didn't budge. I'd missed enough schooling. I considered running away. I was having a full-blown anxiety attack. It wasn't only going back to school feeling inferior and ill-equipped. It had much to do with the anxiety from worrying how Mum would manage alone at home. It was a losing battle. My determined mother took me back to school, got me admitted, and literally escorted me into the classroom, handing me over to the teacher. My classmates had finished three-quarters of the syllabus, and there I was, expected to bounce back as if I'd never been away. I called up the words of Edgar Guest, swallowed hard, and accepted my fate.

It wasn't as bad as I feared. I had one thing going for me as always: I wasn't afraid to work hard. I hunkered down and made it through. Before long, the school term ended, and with it came prize distribution day, with an assembly of 2,000 parents, pupils and other family, friends, teachers, and board members. I was beyond pleased that I'd made it to the finish line. I was content to sit and daydream amid the festivities. Then a classmate poked me with her shoulder.

"Jill," she whispered.

"What?"

"They called out your name!"

I was about to say she was mistaken when I heard it too.

My nerves hit. I wondered what I'd done wrong. I heard my name again—and more.

"Jillian Haslam, please come forward and collect the progress prize for class Five E."

Me? Progress prize? In a daze I floated towards the stage, so dazed I tripped on the stairs, but recovered to receive my prize: a copy of

the book *Twenty Thousand Leagues Under the Sea*. I was stunned and thrilled. It was one of the greatest moments of my life. As I walked off the stage, I caught my mother's eye and saw a face I had not seen in memory, a visage radiating sheer happiness, pure love, and boundless pride. I have never forgotten that look. It filled me with great joy. Mum knew what I had been through and what it meant to get that prize. It was more than a book; it was a life lesson linked to a moment shared between my precious mother and me.

Unknown to me, something else was soon to happen to shape me in profound ways.

11 | My Coat of Many Colors

When we were taken home on the rare occasion for holidays, we didn't have the money to buy much of anything, barely enough for what we needed to survive. Our resourceful and pragmatic mother, however, refused to accept that fate. She always strove to find a solution for life's problems.

In December, for example, she worked her magic when Donna visited and bemoaned the absence of a festive spirit. Mum was good with her hands, like stitching, knitting, or crocheting, and used her skills to make Christmas tree ornaments. She scoured the remains of a demolished building for small bathroom tiles. She then gathered old Christmas cards from friends and cut out the Father Christmas, snowman, or the angels. She glued the cutouts to the tiles, and with paper on the back, fastened a ribbon to the edges to hang them on the discarded imitation trees she'd save. We used those tiles each year.

She applied her wares to more practical purposes as well. Because we'd left Dum Dum with virtually nothing, we needed new clothes but lacked the funds to get them. When our clothes tore or developed holes, she'd of course repair them herself. When we needed clothes

or school uniforms, she'd go to a local tailor—whom she referred to as a master tailor—and ask him as a favor to stitch our school uniforms or a frock each for us. But the biggest find was when she followed him to the back of his shop one day to discover a plentiful array of discarded clothing pieces. To the tailor, they were unusable scraps; to Mum, they were the makings of clothes for her children. And so, a familiar sight was Mum returning home with her arms overflowing with scraps of different cloth. She'd sometimes have Vanessa and I return to the tailor with plastic bags to collect the cloth she couldn't carry. It didn't matter that most of the scraps came from men's shirts and trousers. The material was a treasure trove of colors to use. Vanessa and I were thrilled by the prospects of wearing such splendid clothes.

It quickly became a family project. Vanessa and I, under Mum's watchful supervision, were assigned to separate large pieces from small ones, stained from usable ones, the squares from the triangles, and to segregate colors. Once the material was organized, she'd stitch patchwork quilts, pillowcases, curtains, and, because we couldn't afford proper outer garment and uniforms, jackets and coats made of rectangles of plain colors, each with a collar and lapels made from a patterned material. I have some today. Their handiwork also inspired the establishment of tailoring centers in Calcutta, where scraps of cloth become clothes for the neediest.

Because of all the separation, we deeply cherished our time together. Our parents made it a point to find activities we could share. Even more fun that our communal tailoring tasks were taken up on those rare Sunday mornings when we'd have electricity. Our father would get out an old cassette player with unboxed tapes and play songs like *Coat of Many Colors, A Pink Toothbrush and a Blue Toothbrush, Bimbo,*

Blanket on the Ground, Chicken Every Sunday, and *57 Chevrolet.* Among them all, *Coat of Many Colors,* on a tape of Dolly Parton songs, became my treasured memory.

I'd sit on the floor, leaning back on the bed surrounded by a rainbow of snippets of cloth, while the family listened to Dolly Parton, who because of her background and music played a huge part in our lives. Parton lived in one part of the world and we another, but we related entirely to what she experienced growing up. We had common ground.

The patchwork coats of many colors my mother made for us

My mother also would regale us with her wonderful storytelling skills. No matter what the tale, she had us glued to her every word. Listening to her stories allowed us to enter whatever world she chose to take us and for a short while leave our own. Sometimes we'd lose electricity mid-story and we'd scramble for a candle to light and press Mum to continue. I never wanted the stories to end.

I remember fondly a story Mum told us one Christmas. We'd finished the Christmas tile and decoration making ritual and the

children were sitting on a mat around Mum while she stitched little patchwork coats. Our father was sitting on the bed. Mother announced she'd treat us to a bible story about Jacob and his sons, also called the Coat of Many Colors, but first wanted to take a break for some tea, which she asked me to make. I sighed. I was all warm and cozy on the mat and knew a cup of tea on the old stove would take forever. But of course, I obliged. Once the tea was ready, she began.

"Jacob was an important man who lived in the desert. One day with his family he took his camel, sheep, and goats to a new place called the Land of Canaan. Today it is called Israel. When Jacob settled there, it became the land of the Jews. That was more than three thousand years ago."

"Was Daddy around then?" asked Vanessa, drawing merciless tickling from our father.

"Stop it you two! I want to hear the story!" I shouted, and our mother continued.

"Jacob had a large family. There was his wife, his sons and daughters, and their husbands and wives and children. And there were his servants and their wives and children, too. All were considered a part of the family, but Jacob was especially proud of his twelve sons. One of which was called …?"

"Joseph!" We shouted together.

"Very good," said our father, "that deserves a tickle!" This time I got tickled too, trying not to giggle so I could listen to the story.

"When Joseph was seventeen years old, he had become Jacob's favorite son. Joseph often would snitch to his father about his brother's evil deeds. He was handsome and good, and his father made him …?"

"A coat of many colors!" shouted Vanessa while I looked at my father to warn him no tickling. He grinned but stayed in place.

"When Joseph's brothers saw this beautiful coat, they became jealous. They knew how much more their father loved their brother.

Then Joseph told his brothers about two dreams he had. In one dream he and his brothers were gathering wheat in the field, tying the long stalks into bundles. So, what happened Jillu?"

"Joseph's bundle of wheat stood right up but the others fell over," I promptly responded, "and don't dare tickle me, Daddy!"

He reached out his hands and then stopped, smiling at our mother. She gathered up a piece of bright blue cloth to attach to a yellow one and continued.

"Now, the brothers thought Joseph was saying how much better and important he was, and this made them even more angry. Then Joseph told them about the second dream. The sun and the moon and eleven stars had all bowed down to him and the brothers thought he wanted to rule over them and boss them around. They now were more jealous of him than ever.

"The other brothers wanted to kill Joseph, but the oldest brother ...?"

"Reuben!" I shouted, getting carried away. I ended up being chased by my father's wiggling fingers—there was no space for us to chase each other around the room—as he tried to display anger, but mostly giggled at the same time. After another tickle, he let me sit down on the floor again.

My mum took the opportunity to say, "now that your father has interrupted the story, please warm up the remaining tea and bring me a cup." Oh! I wished we could have the story without so many distractions. I got Mum a refill and we continued.

"Reuben did not want Joseph to be killed and he begged his brothers not to do it. He said they should put him in a deep well instead and Reuben would return later and help Joseph get out. But while Reuben was gone, the other brothers saw a camel caravan that was going to Egypt and they sold Joseph to the leader of the caravan for twenty pieces of silver. Now poor Joseph was a slave. The brothers then dipped Joseph's coat of colors in goat blood and

showed it to their father, who assumed that Joseph had been torn apart by wild beasts.

"Remember girls, it is better that we take care of and love each other and never do each other harm. We want to stay together."

And so that is how the sessions tended to go, our mother's captivating words interspersed with tickles and banter and wisdom. The atmosphere, frolicking, tales, and all, represented magical times, a much-needed respite from the world around us. They were rare occasions when we functioned as a normal family, suspending all emotional and physical pain or troubles we had. And even though I often had boils on my face and all over my body because of the heat in summer, the sheer joy of those family gatherings, the love, the peace, and the hope, anesthetized the pain and discomfort I had. I wish I could have freeze-framed the feeling.

And then there was the outing, different from all the others, which is a memory forever embedded within me. One early morning, Mum took Vanessa and me to a food bank run by the Sisters of Charity. After a long trek, we waited in the heat for hours in a line that snaked beyond where the eye could see. There were thousands of people, each waiting patiently for their share of unknown charitable offerings. I was about nine at the time, and it escaped me why we were going to such extraordinary trouble for what I assumed would be a mere pittance.

When Vanessa and I finally reached the front of the queue, after a four-hour wait, standing in front of us, handing out packets, was Mother Teresa. She gave us biscuits and a little pat on the cheek. I stared into her eyes, riveted. I felt this enveloping power coming from her. Then, as quickly, we were ushered from the line. Walking away, I couldn't take my eyes off her, trying to keep her in sight over my shoulder as Mum rushed us to return home. As a young girl, I didn't know that this woman who had everyone's attention was a larger-than-life persona, but the magnitude of her presence overwhelmed

me. It was unlike anything I'd experienced in a human being. I didn't know what it meant, only that it had a grip on me. And I for sure didn't know that many years later Mother Teresa and I would have a different kind of life intersection.

12 | The Milk of Human Kindness

Hours passed without me noticing anything except the ticking of our rusty alarm clock. It was early February 1980 and eight months before my tenth birthday, and the temperature was a comfortable twenty-four degrees Celsius, a heat I could usually sleep soundly in. Not today. My mind rattled too much and so I rose to start the day. To avoid wakening Vanessa, I quietly scurried around the room, sweeping, cleaning, and folding and refolding a blanket for a bed. I even mopped the outside veranda as best I could. Once done, I sat in my father's chair, a rickety piece of twisted iron. My bare feet scarcely touched the cracked floor.

In our tiny room, we had a single shelf, high on the wall, attached to the dirty, white-painted concrete. It was where we stored precious items. Among them was the small torch someone gave Dad, the pretty handkerchiefs Mum took huge delight in receiving on birthdays, and the odd cracked ornament grateful neighbors passed on as a thank you.

Below the shelf and above the bed was a little altar, two eight-by-eleven-inch pictures: one of Jesus, the other of Our Lady Mary. We were not particularly religious, but we did pray at night, beseeching

for the health and happiness of our matrons, teachers, parents, siblings, and neighbors, and of course each other. We parroted the Lord's prayer, taking comfort in the reference to daily bread, no matter how empty our bellies.

This day I kept a vigil eye on the doorway, eagerly hoping for any sound that announced the return of our parents. My pregnant mother had left several days ago to give birth, my dad half carrying her to the free hospital several miles away. The look on her exhausted face haunted my dreams when I half dozed earlier, trying to conjure up a best-case scenario but all the while fearing the worst.

The free hospital was where the poorest of the poor got treated and gave birth. It was the best option for Mummy and the baby to survive. I squeezed my eyes shut, hoping against hope, but the thought of Mummy not coming home nibbled at the edges of my mind. That could never happen. Could it?

No.

None of us could cope without Mum.

Vanessa awoke. She wanted to help and offered to scrub the utensils, trying her best to take some of the load off me. She, too, was exhausted from anticipation. I'd given up trying to rest. Each time I'd closed my eyes, the distant cry of a baby, from a nearby room, turned into the echo of my eldest sister Donna's screams five years ago. Her anguished cries, at the sight of our twin baby brother Alan and sister Kimberley being placed inside tea chests for burial, were sounds I'd longed to forget. But never have. Never will.

After the burial, I overheard Mummy telling friends that doctors warned her about having more children. But pregnancy, either wanted or unwanted, was part of God's will. I prayed and prayed it wouldn't lead to Mummy's death.

When she left for the hospital this time, she reassured me she wouldn't be long as she winced and waddled off into the night, with Dad propping her up. She never wanted us to worry. Her mantra was

THE MILK OF HUMAN KINDNESS

consistent: there is someone worse off than you. And in the slums, she was right.

But she also never wanted us to go without. Every night she insisted we eat whatever food she'd found that day, claiming she was full because someone or the other had fed her earlier. As her shadow disappeared down the streets a few days ago, I had looked at her matchstick-like legs, worried that they could easily snap, barely able to prop up her weight.

Why weren't they home yet?

As dawn broke, I continued to stare at the passage as the daily familiar sounds and smells of the slum slowly filtered into our space.

First, the fire next door got lit. Didi, the Hindi name for sister, Mum's best friend, always rose at 4 a.m. to light a fire to cook her husband's *subzi* and *roti*—vegetable curry and bread made with flour—for his lunch before he set off for work. The smoke seeped under our door and through wall cracks. Vanessa coughed in response. We were long used to coughing in the morning. It never bothered us. Dad even sang a silly little ditty about it.

"Oh, Didi's frying again and Didi's frying again. It's 4 o'clock in the morning and Didi's frying again."

I smiled at the thought of Dad's daft song. It never failed to make us giggle first thing. I cleared my throat as the familiar tickle enveloped my nostrils. Quietly, so I didn't wake Vanessa after she'd nodded off again, I opened the door to let fresh air dilute the acrid smoke.

Next came the cheerful cry of the drain lady as other early risers shouted their good mornings to each other. With her bare hands and a piece of tin, she always picked up whatever delights the drain held to throw into a bucket with a flourish.

Next came the giggles of toddlers chasing each other up and down the slender lane, so narrow you could touch both sides with barely outstretched arms.

In the distance, I heard a street vendor chasing street kids away, probably throwing a piece of samosa or bread at them before he set up for the day.

Beyond, I could hear the clinking noise of buckets and the sound of the water pump as men started to brush their teeth with neem sticks and clear their throats.

Familiar sounds we'd grown to love, signifying the start of a fresh day before the incessant cacophony of a busy slum overwhelmed the air.

Suddenly Didi stuck her head inside our doorway.

"Any news, Jillu, about Memsaab?" She asked. She was smiling but her forehead was knotted with concern. Like all the neighbors, she called Mum *Memsaab*, meaning Ma'am.

Her voice snapped my consciousness fully back into the room.

"Not yet," I replied. My face was burning, my habitual fever reaction to an anxious event.

"Ah stay strong, God will never abandon us," Didi said, beaming the brightest of smiles. Her positivity lit up our room. She glanced at our altar. "God never gives you more than you can deal with. Stay strong, Jillu, they'll be home soon," she said. I returned the smile and off she went, chuckling to herself, her arms full of washing.

Vanessa woke again, rubbing her eyes, staring at me.

"Are they not back yet?"

"No," I replied, holding back tears.

As if Didi had known, the doorway suddenly filled with Dad's stooping shoulders, Mummy clinging to his elbow. I opened my mouth to speak but stopped myself. He held a bunch of blankets in the crook of his arm.

"You're back!" I cried.

Neither answered.

One look told me all I needed to know. Dad turned to help shuffle my mum to the bed. Wordlessly, she crawled under a blanket and curled into a fetus shape. With no more than a whisper, she told

us the doctors gave the baby about three days to live. Dad placed the bundle next to her and slumped into his chair.

They looked like broken souls.

"They sent us home, Jillu." He whispered. "They say she won't survive."

His voice was flat and dull, emitting a tone I'd never heard from him before. I looked at Mum, her face an impassive mask. She tried to speak to me, I assume to offer some comfort like she did about everything bad, but no sound escaped. Vanessa, mute with shock, stood there speechless.

Without asking, I took the few short steps to the bed. I moved the motionless bundle of blankets apart to see a peaceful, almost emaciated face nestled inside. Loosening her swaddle, I gently pulled out a tiny hand and tiny foot, the skin as soft as fine sand.

"She is so beautiful, Mummy," I smiled. She looked so perfect. It was hard to believe she was dying. I marveled at how precious she was, feeling a proud swell of love in my heart for my new baby sister.

Then she opened her eyes.

They were sunken and glazed. They told me she might never grow to see anything outside these walls. I knew the look of malnourishment.

I picked up Neil so he could see her and gave her a little kiss on her cheek.

Dad was bent double in his chair, head in hands. He usually held himself erect and proud, his sparse hair neatly combed, dressed in a shirt and trousers. The discipline he'd learned in the British Army never left him, even in a Calcutta slum. Tufts stuck up from behind his ears and his rumpled shirt wasn't fully tucked.

"Jillu, your sister has been born with rickets." He said slowly. "It is a disease caused by a lack of vitamin D, calcium, and other things. You can tell by looking at her with her swollen belly, her tiny thin … " His weak voice trailed off.

Dad never hid the truth from us, always careful to explain. He wanted us to grow up understanding our situation in an educated manner. Often, he used metaphors from philosophers, poets, singers, and writers to illustrate his points. We could quote Einstein, Kipling, and various British greats from the time we could speak. Even if we didn't know exactly what the words meant, they comforted us.

Mummy let out a noise that sounded like a sob from somewhere deep inside.

"I have lost my other babies and this will happen again," as if speaking to no one but herself. She took a deep breath, before turning her face to the mattress.

Instinctively and carefully, I picked up the bundle. In my mind's eye, I suddenly saw Donna again, hunched over the tea chest, sobbing her heart out at seeing her baby twin siblings die. I was too young to fully understand what had happened back then. Afterwards, I had wondered if all babies went off to live in tea chests.

Now, almost ten years old, I understood Donna's pain. As she loved those twins, I loved this baby already. It was a deep protective love that surprised me.

"We can help her," I whispered to Dad urgently. "Feed her milk. Stop her from starving."

He shook his head with such helplessness and sadness that my stomach knotted. I knew in that moment he didn't get the advance he'd asked from his boss. What little money we had wouldn't stretch far. I felt heat rising in my head again. But I didn't want to be unwell. I needed to be strong to help. I wiped my forehead, relieved Dad seemed too upset to notice. He might have told me to put the baby down otherwise.

"What's her name?" I asked.

"Susan," Mum replied.

"That's lovely," said Vanessa, peering at our new sister with pride similar to my own.

Susan was the name of a tall, beautiful teacher (the daughter of our food matron at boarding school) who helped us whenever she could. She was consistently kind, gentle, and respectful to my mother. The perfect person to name a baby after.

Mum reached for her with shaking arms and I carefully placed her on the bed. Mum was too weak to grab the baby from me.

"She's going to die, Jillu," she said gently. "We can't stop this. We just have to be here for her."

Tears formed in my eyes, making Mum's face fuzzy. Vanessa was openly crying now. I tried to keep my rising tears in.

"We must accept Susan may not make it. All we can do is make her as comfortable as possible, show her she was blessed. There is a reason she's been sent to our family so we will show her love and care," Dad continued weakly. "The doctor gave us this medicine but I doubt it can do any good. She needs it every hour, mixed with milk. But Mummy can't make milk and we can't afford what we need."

I took the small white envelope of paper he pointed to and held it to my chest. Inside were white tablets with instructions to grind, mix with a teaspoon of milk, then give to the baby. It was a glimmer of hope. The doctors had still given them something, hadn't they? They wouldn't have done that if she were destined to die would they?

Poor Mummy's eyes closed as weakness overcame her. I felt a surge of desperation to turn this situation around. I wanted to make Mum happy. I wanted to save my sister Susan, who had been handed a death sentence before she'd even drunk milk.

Milk!

Something so simple was the answer. Babies drank milk and she needed it more than ever now. It was her only chance. My only chance.

I carefully rearranged Susan's blankets, so they didn't fall over, then without saying where I was going, I put on my mother's slippers and darted out of our door. Spying a stainless-steel bowl washed up on our veranda, I grabbed it and tore down the passage towards

the vendors. My head spun with thoughts as I zigzagged as fast as I could down the narrow corridors, jumping over neighbors throwing buckets of water out, avoiding kids playing with a broken plastic ball. All I could think about was milk, milk, milk!

The vendors who sold food to the extremely poor of the slums worked a few minutes from our front door. They cooked from tiny places, in the street over large coal fires, using woks to fry sweets or dry fry rotis or provide tea and samosas. Vanessa and I had tried and true methods of extracting food from vendors, a combination of unabashed persistence and patience. But today it wasn't food I needed; it was milk. And it wasn't to fill a belly; it was to save a life.

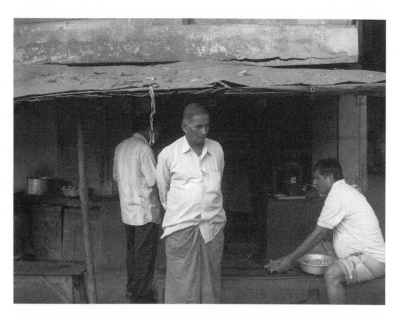

The tea shop that gave me the free milk that helped me to save Susan's life

My new target was the tea shop.

A grumpy, middle-aged vendor called Ashok ran the small tea shop. We often worked for him, shifting to the bin the piles of ash that accumulated underneath his huge clay ovens. For that filthy

unpleasant job, he'd pay us in stale biscuits or any unsold food that was left for days. I'd never asked for milk before. Now I wondered what mood he was in.

Before reaching the tea shop, because I was so eager, I clumsily knocked into a man on a bicycle. He yelled at me but I didn't miss a beat of my run. When I arrived in front of Ashok, I was panting like an exhausted dog.

"Go away," he spat without even looking up from the dirty glass counter that displayed small sweets. In front of the stall sat two old benches for customers to sit on, next to an old metal drum of water where people could wash their hands and rinse their mouths. I took a deep breath before words tumbled out.

"Please-Ashok-I-need-some-milk," I said as if in one word.

He smiled, revealing red and brown teeth. For a split second, I wanted to hug him as it looked as if he would fill the bowl I held out, mimicking a scene out of Oliver Twist.

"Ha-ha! You want milk? Get lost. You'll be wanting half the shop next."

I knew Ashok had heard this all before, hundreds of times a week.

People brought their children with cleft palates, their husbands without legs, their starving pregnant wives, all begging for a small meal, one mouthful to save them from certain or near death. In desperate times, people took desperate measures.

"Ashok it's not for me, it's for Susan," I said, forcing myself to speak slower. "She's my new baby sister. She'll die without it."

He looked at me in disbelief.

"Ah really?" He questioned. "Go home to your parents and that naughty sister of yours."

But Ashok knew I wasn't lying about having a new baby in the family. After all, my mother had shuffled past him when she returned from the hospital. He also knew I was trustworthy. I'd never stolen from him or asked for more than was fair.

Ashok nodded at a waiting customer, indicating our conversation was over. I stood with a racing mind, wondering what I could say next to persuade him. I positioned myself neatly to the side, watching like a hawk.

We had in the past endured burning splashes of hot fat for hours for a piece of food. The least I could do now for Susan was stand here, despite my naturally shy nature. So I waited, humming to myself, swaying from foot to foot as Ashok pointedly ignored me.

An hour passed and I remained in the same spot. Several times Ashok tried to shoo me away, but I stood firm. When the buzz of the shop died down, he glanced up and caught my eye. This time he held my gaze with more interest.

"So, you say you have a baby sister?' he said, more gently. "She's dying? Who says so?"

"The doctors and my parents," I said, unable to take my eyes off the huge *dachi* of milk bubbling on the on the fire. "Please, Ashok, I can't let her die. Please give me some milk so I can feed her."

He snatched my stainless-steel bowl and smoothly filled it up with a ladle. It looked thinner in smaller portions, possibly diluted eight to one, but I couldn't stop smiling. It was liquid gold.

"Now get out." He bellowed. "And don't come back!"

"Thank you!" I exclaimed, turning as quickly and carefully as possible. I needed to get home fast, without wasting a precious drop.

Back home, the room was so deathly quiet nobody could have guessed a newborn baby had arrived.

"I have milk, Mummy!" I said triumphantly.

My exhausted parents exchanged startled looks before Dad quickly stood to help crush the tablets to mix with the milk. I took a spoon, squeezed Susan's cheeks, and gently dribbled tiny amounts in-between her thin lips, now a worrying shade of dark grey. Some pooled into the corners of her mouth but she gently sucked on the rest to my absolute relief.

My mother began to cry. I thought they were tears of happiness, but later realized they probably were from fear of harboring unrealistic hopes. Susan drank as much as she could, before closing her eyes.

As I rocked my baby girl back to sleep, I gently pressed my nose to her forehead breathing in her sweet baby smell. Silently I made a promise to do everything I could to save her. After laying her down, I picked up the rusty alarm clock to set the timer for the next hour. I was so tired. But I had to plan ahead, which I would do for nights on end.

I vowed silently to return to Ashok tomorrow and the next day and the next. Even if I had to beg for his kindness, I'd do whatever it took. I'd work extra hours for him. I'd get there early. I'd even offer to take the job of the little boy who washed his utensils. Just if he'd let me have the milk. Somehow, I was determined there would be a miracle and Susan would survive. That was my hope, and I clung to it.

We never had much but we always had hope. And I knew without hope in the slums you have nothing.

Finally, I allowed my heavy eyelids to close. With my intention to save Susan, I let myself relax again.

Little did I realize then, I'd found something precious, deep inside of myself. My strong willpower to make something happen made me more likely to succeed. I decided on a clear path to follow and nothing was going to stop me. Call it mind over matter, the power of intent, or whatever you like. But it's something I live by today, as much as my nine-year-old self did, holding my dying sister, back then.

13 | Life at the Bottom

Each day, in teeny increments, Susan gained essential strength. I had become a surrogate at home, with my father often at work and my mother struggling with her recovery. My mother had relented to let me stay home to care for my younger siblings—and, without it said, to look after her as well. She agreed Vanessa could stay and help me. School was again on hold.

When my mother got better, she began venturing into Calcutta each day, searching for work, food, or whatever help she could garner. Freeing her up that way normalized my role bringing up both small children with Vanessa at my side.

Things got complicated when the landlord unexpectedly hit us with a 10 percent rent raise. The initial jolt from this development was bad enough. Worse was that my parents couldn't afford the increase. As soon as that became clear, the landlord began harassing us. He sometimes locked us out of our home, verbally abused my father, kicked our buckets of water over, spat in our house, and even raised his hands to my father. To try and buy some time and preserve his health, my father eventually had to return to live with friends in the

city. My mother implored the landlord to cease his antics, explaining that my father had taken ill, hoping he would allow us to live in the room until my parents could find a solution to the problem.

My father eventually returned, despite the fact the landlord had been entirely unforgiving and uncompromising. By that time, the unpaid portion of the rent had ballooned, prompting the landlord to start charging interest on the rent arrears and demanding rent be paid on time.

Our home situation was tenuous. Each morning I'd kiss my father goodbye on his way to work, and he'd say, "Hold the fort, Jillu. We all have our crosses to carry, and ours are much lighter than what others have. Carry it with pride, and remember, there is a reason for everything that happens in life."

He was fond of that phrase, "crosses to bear." It equalized the playing field emotionally and helped us accept whatever struggles faced us. His cross, however, seemed to be getting far too heavy. I could see changes in him. He had noticeably less zip and seemed increasingly exhausted. He didn't joke as much. His eyes had no glow and were almost dull. I began to worry.

Then it happened. He suffered another heart attack—his third. We couldn't care for him at home and lacked resources for medications and hospital care, so he moved in with a friend in the city again to gain strength and heal. That meant the end of his job, ratcheting up pressure on the rest of us. We each were stretched to capacity. Sometimes my mother would be out from morning darkness until evening darkness, and with little food, we had to await her return amid uncertainty. We didn't have a phone and normally didn't know where she'd gone. There was literally no way to contact her if an emergency or problem with the little ones arose.

She wanted us to believe that when not doing odd jobs, she was making the rounds with better-off friends to pick up food offerings for us. The truth was, we later learned, she only called on a single

couple for help, Mr. Neil and his wife, Mrs. Joyce O'Brien. Mr. Neil O'Brien served on various educational boards, including at our school, and was also a member of Parliament. He helped hundreds of families survive and make something of themselves. The O'Briens held my mother in high regard and felt we were blessed to have her. They were a huge help to us.

My mother developed a patchwork survival manual. Sometimes she got food from friends. Sometimes she made money working. Sometimes she borrowed money from friends. Sometimes she persuaded a local butcher to part with meat on credit. She even pawned our transistor radio for twenty rupees to buy vegetables, pay bills, and conjure up a tiny meal. She did what she could do. She was relentless.

That left the full agenda of domestic chores to Vanessa and me, in addition to watching over Neil and Susan. In the afternoons, after we put the little ones to sleep, Vanessa and I sometimes went to a local tea shop after the merchant had put out the huge fire in the clay oven. He allowed us to collect the hot ashes and bring them home to clean dishes since we lacked money for detergent. Vanessa and I made a game out of it, competing to see who could make their dishes shine the brightest.

We sometimes got burnt from the hot ash we picked up from the oven, but we carried on and let nothing dampen our spirits. We would pretend we were making dal-puris—the delicious snack everybody eats for breakfast in West Bengal. I would scrub the dishes as though I was putting lentils in the puris, and after I put them in the bucket of water, Vanessa would rinse them as if frying the food. We'd mimic the local restaurant cooks and talk in a rough tone and have lots of fun, sometimes play-instructing Neil and Susan around to get orders from imaginary customers.

I remember how we struggled washing our 6'2" tall father's trousers. His pants were so large and we were very tiny and we had to hold the clothes-washing brush in our hands while running up and

down his trousers. Like the mice in the movie Cinderella, trying to wash something many times their size, we would take hold of both sides and squeeze and squeeze with all our tiny might trying to rinse them. We never quite got it right. We were too weak to wring enough water out and the pants were too heavy to lift and hang to dry. We stood on a cane stool stacked on top of a large tin and held each other until we could reach the washing line to put them out to dry—sometimes falling over, hitting our heads, saving each other, laughing non-stop, and sometimes crying from

The clothes line in front of our little room

bruises and scratches and huge bumps on our heads given that the ground and the drain and the ledge were all concrete. The clothes line sometimes broke and after falling over we often had all of the filth from the drain stuck to our hair, but we still soldiered on for the sake of the little ones.

Being alone also had a dark side.

Because our parents were usually gone during the day, the landlord—who we always seemed to owe money—liked to come by and ask about our parents and cast his eyes about to make sure we were alone. He'd make us dance for him to a song from the famous Indian movie *Sholay* and role-play the characters played by Bollywood

actors Hema Malini and Dharmendra. After our performance, he'd give us sweets, a Coca Cola to share, corn on the cob, or other food from local vendors who passed by, but not without trying to touch us first. Being hungry most of the time, we didn't mind the dancing if it meant getting something to eat and share with the younger ones. Even other men gathered to watch. Many times, all we heard was, "Hey, white rat," he'd say in Hindi, "come here and dance for us!"

The touching confused us. There were always several men wanting to behave inappropriately. We were hungry and alone and didn't understand that their behavior was mean and violative. Did they clap because we were partially naked and they were depraved, or because they liked us as kids or how we danced? The reality for us was that we did what we had to do to survive. I often asked my father why men tried to touch us. He always answered the same.

"What you need to remember is that our destiny should not be preordained by the color of our skin or the country of our ancestors. Yet, unfortunately, in the fickle world we live in, those things have a huge influence over various outcomes. You need to rise above that. That's what strength is all about. People say and do things in ignorance. Believing or accepting it and allowing it to influence your future makes you ignorant, too; you need to make that decision. We should pity these people and not hate them."

Where we lived crawled with poor and illiterate men. Perhaps they didn't grasp how their behavior impacted young minds. Regardless, they didn't seem to care or know better. Vanessa sometimes dealt with it more than I. She was fairer-skinned and blond, a more inviting target. But we both endured the abuse. Because of the heat and humidity, we often wore only panties, which we got from the Sisters of Charity. More often than not they were adult knickers, which started above our waists and ended well below our knees. The crotch portion was typically black due to the time we spent on the ground washing dishes and clothes or walking in the mud carrying water. We

walked around as if we were rich. To us, the knickers were a gift beyond imagination. To lecherous men, they were a magnet for mischief.

Being victimized by local men was but one of many dangers we faced. Our daily chores teemed with hazards. We used to fill plastic buckets with water from a handpump quite a distance away. We had to walk in ankle-deep mud, all the more slippery because of our bare feet. Sometimes we wore rubber slippers but they made it more dangerous

The communal area in Kidderpore

when walking with buckets of water or utensils. The buckets of water and wet laundry we carried weighed us down, sometimes causing us to stumble or fall, spill the contents, and return to refill the buckets and re-rinse our clothes.

Sometimes crying, occasionally bleeding, laughing here and there, and every now and then plain angry, we'd carry on, day after day. Later, a pump got installed closer to home, which helped, but it had a tiny area around it where men came to bathe, women to wash clothes and utensils, and children to use as a toilet. We slipped many a time into the drain—bucket, clothes, utensils, and all—and got hurt, but we didn't have the time or luxury to worry about it. We had two little ones at home who depended on us. We had to limit our time away and when we came home, we had to be strong in front of them. We didn't want to inject more negativity or dark clouds into their lives than already existed.

I remember once cooking stew and rice, into which I had put much effort. I began in the morning and finished around 7 p.m. I prepared everything on a tiny kerosene stove. The flame was so small it took hours to get the food remotely hot only to have the fuel run out preventing the wicks to light. This tended to occur because the kerosene was diluted with water, which stiffened the wicks. I had to push the wicks up manually, which induced blisters on my fingers. It was an excruciating task getting the food to a decent temperature.

The younger ones were eager to eat and kept asking me if the food was ready. Overtired and exhausted with chores of the day, I picked up the round aluminum pot of hot stew, holding it with both hands using a rag, and as I walked from the veranda into the room, I stumbled and dropped the whole vessel of stew all over myself and onto the floor.

I became instantly deflated; it was a deeply sad moment. My heart sank further when I saw the immediate devastation on the kids' faces, frozen in horror as they stared at the ruined meal. The poor things had not had a single morsel to eat all day and they had waited with great anticipation for this meal—and I ruined it. I didn't care about my burns. I was demoralized for letting them down.

We quickly gathered up the bits of stew off the floor and set them aside while I cleaned the floor—where we'd chase rats away every day—and then sat and ate the food anyway with great relish and not a care in the world. We even left some for our parents. After the meal, I cleaned the entire room again to remove whatever remnants I could of the splattered gravy and vegetables. I wanted to minimize the temptation of cockroaches and vermin to pay us a nightly visit and party at our expense. I scrubbed every nook and cranny.

That night I sobbed from sheer emotional and physical exhaustion, while Vanessa applied cream and blew on my burns, and tried to calm me down before Mum and Daddy got home. I wanted to fall asleep and not wake up for a long time. I wanted to disappear.

14 | Tales of Darkness and Light

One morning, while washing things on our veranda, I heard a frantic call of "Jillu! Jillu!" I looked up to a horrific sight. A lady who lived in the sixth little room at the end of the lane, with panic in her face, had Susan by the arm. Barely more than a toddler at this point, Susan had pieces of coal hanging off her skin and her dress was completely stuck to her. She was bleeding profusely and I could see her ribs as she struggling to breathe and seemed in shock.

Earlier in the day, the woman holding Susan had allowed Neil, Susan, and her two children to ride an old broken tricycle. Because we didn't have access to parks or other places to play, they'd take turns cycling up and down a narrow building passageway nearby. The children evidently pushed her while playing and the tricycle tipped and tumbled over into a pot of boiling water that sat atop a clay oven in the neighbor's veranda. The pot of boiling water, along with the hot coals, toppled over onto her.

I immediately raced to the top of the road to the chemist and begged him frantically for helpful medications. He looked at me and asked about payment. I started crying hysterically. When he saw the

torrent of tears streaming down my cheeks, he told me he had a few expired tubes of Burnol, a medicine used for burns. I grabbed them, dropping a few in my urgency to get home.

When we removed Susan's dress, her skin peeled off. She was burned almost to the bone. Vanessa and I gently soothed the medicine onto her little body and continued to blow on her skin in a feeble attempt to keep her cool. Susan screamed on and on and then suddenly stopped responding. We needed Mum but had no way of reaching her. I felt helpless and, down deep felt a fear and panic that told me I wasn't old enough to manage the situation. We tried to calm her down but the injury was far too serious. I began to cry.

We did what we could until Mum returned. She sent someone to get a rickshaw. It took forever, or that is how it seemed, but we got Susan to the nearest hospital where a friend of my mother named Uncle Jimmy worked. Jimmy kindly paid the rickshaw and got medical staff to give us immediate attention. They wound up bandaging her from shoulders to hips. The poor thing had to be in unbearable pain.

The bond I had developed with Susan when she was an infant meant she was the most precious thing in the world to me and the thought she might die from this horrific accident terrified me. She survived yet again, and heaven only knows how and why. She was a fragile child and had little flesh on her body, but thousands of tears, plenty of prayers, and a tremendous amount of love saw her through another devastating ordeal.

The burn scare with Susan was another sharp reminder—of many—about appreciating the little things in life. Love of family, community kindness, and empathy had become our core values: the most precious assets we had. Everything else was detail.

We crammed our entire universe into that tiny room in Kidderpore. We had our clothes and books and things for cooking and a handful of plastic bags with tailor scraps and rags. We were—

by necessity of course—minimalists. If anything, the way we lived, we probably had *too* many things. Take one step inside the room and you could sit down on the single bed we had.

To my mother, it was all about community. No surprise, then, that she welcomed into the home several cats and birds she had "rescued." Beyond that, with her heart of gold, she at times brought people home to help them get back on their feet or for a meal. She wanted to help everybody she could. She often said what four can eat, five can too, and we should share what we had with whomever she brought home. At times, it seemed she wanted to bring every animal and person off the street. If she could fill every inch of that room she would.

All the drama aside, my mother knew that a connected and compassionate community instilled a sense of belonging and fueled the human spirit. She wanted to stay focused on the bigger picture. That was all the more important in communities like ours where material possessions were limited and each day was a siege to survive. She was building a value-based culture through our family— sometimes to a fault, considering the menagerie she assembled inside the Kidderpore room—but she was onto something vital about thriving cultures and what makes people shine and prosper spiritually.

What happened to Susan that day on the bike was horrendous. But it was part and parcel of life in the slum. My mother knew we couldn't avoid similar things from happening. We could try to minimize the risks, but we would be foolish if we felt singled out, cursed, or less than others because of how we lived. That wasn't always easy—and I have in mind the lecherous-men aspect of our existence, with more to follow there—but she wanted us to find beauty in our poverty, in the simplicity of our lives, and the human values we could and should commonly embrace.

15 | Suffering in Silence

My entire life in India people looked at us differently. It had nothing to do with a lack of shared beliefs and culture. It was who we were to them, manifested in the differences in our language, ethnicity, and physical features. We were intriguing curiosities at best and targets for ridicule, belittlement, and abuse at worst.

The walk from our little home to the main road where transport like trams, buses, or taxis were available was a good 30-40 minute walk down a road where we would encounter hundreds of young boys or even middle aged men who tried to touch or man-handle us, and made the most vulgar of gestures and signs openly hurling names at us like *sada chua* (white rat), *sada murghi* (white chicken), *sada goo* (white shit), *sada tilchate* (white cockroach), *dasi murghi* (foreign chicken), *randi* (prostitute), and many more. We were constant targets of such vulgarity and sexual advances. For many, it came easy to justify mistreating people deemed beneath them.

Of course, not everyone stooped to that level. At every opportunity, our parents made a point to allow us to mix with decent, respectful, and kind people. When some Indian children played with

us, my father encouraged us to live normally. While he cautioned it would take a while to get used to each other's differences, he encouraged us to appreciate, respect, and honor variations and exalt and celebrate what we had in common.

To help us develop as normal, rounded individuals, our parents urged us to express ourselves and be our own persons, even though female independence was culturally frowned upon—even taboo. For sure, standing up for ourselves was fraught with problems, so much so that my father preferred not to bring us home from school for the holidays. He worried that garden variety verbal abuse and taunting might escalate into serious sexual or physical abuse or even kidnapping. His warnings were ominous.

By the time Donna reached young adulthood, she had blossomed into a sexually attractive and beautiful young woman—and a magnet for the worst kind of attention. Local thugs in Calcutta constantly bugged her, often asking for money. One day, as she was shopping at a local vendor, a voice behind her demanded money. It was a familiar voice, as that same guy had harassed her for money many times before and she, as a defense mechanism, had more often than not obliged him. This time she adamantly refused, tending to her business. He persisted aggressively, triggering her feisty side, and as she turned to start giving him a piece of her mind, he slashed her face with a razor and fled. Being the fighter she was (and is), Donna didn't scream for help but pursued him. Unable to catch him, she rerouted to the police station where, while bleeding, she reported what'd happened, resulting in the man's arrest. Donna later got hospital treatment, but that beast had scarred a young and beautiful girl for life.

Three months later, astonishingly, she forgave the assailant, even giving him some money. He was as poor as we were, if not more so, and Donna had taken to pity him. That day, my older sister laid the groundwork to teach me a courageous lesson about the power

of forgiveness. And while I didn't fully grasp it then, it would take center stage years later in a way I could never have imagined.

Donna wasn't alone in fending off dangerous and evil men.

We often snuck into the building across from our room to eavesdrop on workers creating *saris* to sell. Saris are a traditional garment women wear in India. We'd watch in fascination as they laid plain cloth on long tables and dipped wooden stamps of varying shapes and sizes into color or paint to emblazon the cloth with beautiful designs and patterns.

The business owner took a liking to us and occasionally invited us to watch movies on a small television. My father approved because we were but a few paces from home, which allowed him to check on us from time to time. The owner brightened our days with biscuits and sweets and sometimes even dinner or pocket money. It became our personal sanctuary away from home.

One day while my siblings and I were lying in a row on the table watching a movie, the owner stood to the side and slowly put his hands down my panties. I was maybe eleven and didn't know if this was right or wrong or how to handle it. I froze and looked at him. I imagine I looked innocent and fragile. He smiled at me and at the time I didn't feel hurt. Now, of course, thoughts of the incident disgust me. He was, I should note, one of many men who did such things. We were expected to grin and bear it.

He was an otherwise respectable man, well regarded in the community. He had a wonderful family and treated my parents with decency. They seemed to trust him, which was saying a lot for my father who often withheld trust from people outside the family.

The man's community standing could spell trouble for us if I made a fuss. At a minimum, he'd cut off what help he provided our

family. Saying something would also jeopardize the movies and treats he gave my siblings, things we otherwise only dreamt about. I said nothing and the molestation continued.

At the time, in my young and relatively uninformed mind, I thought silence a small price to pay for everyone's peace of mind. I knew that if the truth came out, I'd have triggered more harm than good. The esteem by which he was held in the community gave him power and influence and the ability to harm us in innumerable ways. Soiling his reputation—or trying to do so—would have been a major misstep with unknown consequences, none good, and maybe even fatal for any one of us.

I may have kept quiet, but I never forgot. The fondling and other inappropriate behavior became increasingly frequent and continued for some time. It got to where I stopped going there altogether, but that indiscrete protective measure luckily didn't bring retribution to my family. My siblings continued to go—the benefits were hard to ignore—but to my knowledge, they were never bothered. I am sure they would have told me.

Stress in the slum came in various other forms, albeit not the same for everyone. Consider one event that for most locals was a source of unbridled fun and celebration and for us a complete disaster.

Holi, the festival of color, observes the advent of spring and signifies the triumph of good over evil where people rejoice by, among other things, spraying each other with colored powder. For us, however, Holi was hardly triumphant. It was feared: a time when groups of louts and bullies descended upon us to heap abuse. Those mini gangs used balloons filled with colored water and laid in wait to attack us. Whenever we came into view, they'd bombard us from high-rise buildings or by running straight towards us from hiding places, pelting us at close range, into our chests, stomachs, backsides, and even faces, laughing as they fled. The close hits often split our skin or caused blisters. Getting pounded in the

face sometimes sent us to the ground and almost always made us dizzy and dazed. Not only were our clothes often ruined but our attackers delighted in slamming balloons against our chests, groins, or backsides to ensure maximum pain and humiliation. Once soaked, our bodies would be visible through the material. We would walk home with one arm over our chests and the other in our laps.

Much as I wanted to hold back tears, I couldn't. It was impossible not to cry. We were shaken and upset. We had no option but to brave the onslaught and continue on to wherever we were headed. Sometimes we'd find a good-hearted woman in the hope she'd intervene, chase them away, or bring us something to wrap ourselves in. We'd occasionally chased the perpetrators, but the massive crowds inevitably swallowed them up.

Each year we feared the impending festival. We knew that even with extra clothes to protect ourselves, and our heads down and shielded, nothing would stop the onslaught. It was a nightmare. We tried to avoid dangerous lanes or places of potential ambush. But once out in the open, we were marked—hundreds of people stared and laughed at us while we were under siege. To most people, it was entertainment at our expense, albeit not something they dared try with an Indian girl.

If we were lucky to have a few rupees, we took a rickshaw to avoid the boys lurking and leering from both sides of the street. Nervous and panicky, we tried to cover up, worried at the thought of them waiting to drench us. Unrelentingly, unashamedly, they ran along side of the rickshaw and pelted us with the water balloons. Our efforts were, at the end of the day, futile. We never could be out in public during those times without getting our clothes wrecked, color everywhere, and injured in body, mind, and heart.

Sometimes the abuse we faced growing up came when and where we least expected.

One day, a truck driver broke my mother's arm when he abruptly opened his door without looking. Susan took her to a free hospital for an X-ray and the X-ray technician offered Susan the chance to press the green button on the machine to start the process. She smiled, thinking how sweet, allowing a little girl worried about her badly injured mother to help with the medical procedure.

But after she pressed the button, he blocked her exit and fondled her breasts before letting her return to my mother. Upset as she was and close to tears, she said nothing, because our mother was in so much pain and also suffering with cancer at the time; the last thing Susan wanted to do was to cause my mum more distress. So, like me, she silently endured.

It wasn't too long after this incident, while Susan was running around with friends near where we lived, that a man in his thirties cornered her. He held her tightly while her friends ran away. She begged him to let her go. After leering at every intimate part of her body, he said in crude Hindi language that he'd let her go. He wanted her to know, however, that some day when she grew up, he'd return to her.

When we were insulted or humiliated in front of my mother, she'd get upset but would say things like, "Let it go, they don't know any better" or, "Does it hurt? Show me where but say nothing. Just leave it because there are too many of them." She believed that if we pushed the envelope, we could be murdered or raped and forgotten about forever, without repercussions. And if we dared impugn a man's reputation, we'd be accused of provoking the behavior.

My father counseled us, saying, "We are among the Philistines, so that's how we must treat them. There's no point in trying to fight,

because if I try to fight one, I'll have a hundred upon me within seconds, and I can't fight them all. If we start a fight, they'll probably murder us all or worse, cause one of you to disappear."

When I think of those days, I recall times when our parents could not contain their hurt or sadness. On a few of those occasions, words got heated, especially when the men had done something particularly awful to us. But I remember us pleading with them, "Dad, Mum! Just leave it. Please don't say anything. Let it go. Let's get home." We were truly terrified of someone harming our parents in front of us after which we'd be abused.

We were learning all about the culture of silence or, some might say, how to "turn the other cheek."

Most of the bad deeds we suffered as children were never brought to the attention of my parents or talked about in their company. Most often, we withdrew and buried the secret, pretending nothing had happened or that something else was bothering us. We shared the accounts and descriptions among us sisters to ensure we knew which men were the worst, whom to stay away or run from ... until the next incident occurred.

16 | Don't Do Unto Others

Diwali, the festival of lights, is celebrated every autumn and one of the most popular festivals of Hinduism. Diwali symbolizes the spiritual victory of light over darkness, good over evil and knowledge over ignorance. It's meaning, however, evaded many in our neighborhood.

I can understand the difficulty for some to accept that light-skinned Anglo-Indians—people of British ancestry—were subject to a regular pattern of abuse. But the truth is, that is the way it was, and the Diwali festival was when the most flagrant and relentless mistreatment occurred.

The Diwali abuser's firework of choice were "chocolate bombs," a makeshift firework made of tiny paperboard boxes stuffed with gunpowder, small nails, and other little metal items, with a fuse inserted in one of the corners. The boxes were tightly wrapped with jute strings, dried in the sun for three days, and then wrapped with colorful aluminum foil, making them look like chocolates. Our tormentors liked to throw them at the passageway in front of our little room and onto our veranda where the bombs would detonate and cause untold havoc.

The bomb detonation was ear-splitting and terrifying, more so when ricocheting within the confined space of our passageway. To brace for the onslaught, we'd lock our sole door and hunker down deep into the room. The reverberation rang in our ears for hours after and our room and the passageway became polluted with smoke and the suffocating smell of burning gunpowder. As evening approached, we remained mummified in that little room, hands over our ears, waiting in dread for the next bomb to land—and praying for an extended respite of silence.

I felt entirely helpless, and I know Vanessa felt the same way. Although Vanessa and I would tightly wrap our arms around little Neil and Susan, the collective noise, one bomb after another, terrorized the kids to the point of trauma. I tremble whenever I recall the all-consuming look of fear on their faces. The attacks were barbaric and merciless, the attackers sadistic. I remember sitting there, tears streaming down my face, holding Susan close to me with my hands over her ears, thinking that one day I'd make sure we'd no longer have to tolerate things like that. Calcutta finally banned the chocolate bomb in 2009.

Chocolate bombs

Another explosive device was the "chilli bomb," an array of hundreds of small red fireworks tied together along a string, sometimes up to twenty feet in length. The abusers would set fire to one end and drop it in front of our little room or on the veranda. The deafening noise that followed would linger non-stop for ten to fifteen minutes. There were times I thought it would never end and we'd be banished to a lifetime of explosions. No sooner had one string burnt

*The passageway in front of our little room where
the chocolate bombs would explode*

out than another would land in front of our little room as we huddled
inside, cowering in a corner and trembling in fear. They would also
send rockets from the necks of bottles that exploded in the room if
we hadn't closed the door in time. Their cruelty wasn't limited to
humans. They treated local dogs the same, setting off explosives tied
to their tails. It was our version of a war zone.

The reign of terror sometimes lasted past Diwali, converting
our little room into a bunker. We dared not leave other than for
essentials. If we did, our assailants would be lying-in-wait, and when
we appeared, they'd pummel us with glee as they watched the bombs
terrorize and burn us or knock us down—all for their amusement.
Their assaults kept us indoors from early afternoon or evening through
the next morning as if we were under sniper fire. We had to pee in a
mug and get rid of it later, afraid to venture outside to the toilet but a
few steps away. Early morning exits were the best bet, but even then
we might encounter one or more of them lounging around.

Those were hard times. Nights, with no ventilation, were unbearably hot with extremely high humidity, but we had to remain boxed in to stay safe and relatively sane. The worst of the bullies tormented us the entire time we lived there. Their behavior was barbarous. Many preyed on us because we were different and poor. Knowing how badly we got unnerved gave them great pleasure. They couldn't care less if the house contained a dying child, a traumatized two-year-old, or a heart patient like my father. We had no means to fight back. We were prisoners in our own home.

I grew to detest the festivals. Recalling the experience today gives me body shudders. We couldn't change the way we looked and had no way of escaping the poverty that gripped us. But as always, our mother gave us the strength to carry on. No matter the degree or source of suffering in our childhood and adolescence, she inspired us to maintain composure and dignity and withstand all negativity and abuse, repeatedly reminding us that gratitude and love rise above all. I absorbed my mother's counsel, even if it didn't always immediately land with me.

The Diwali experiences exacerbated my naturally unmoored self. The smallest things started to unsettle me. I became even more timid. I panicked easily. Loud noises, like a vehicle backfiring, a balloon popping, or the burst of a firecracker at Christmas, startled me. Even today, my family jokes about how easy it is to frighten me when playing around. I craved peaceful, quiet, non-confrontational experiences. I wanted to be alone for long stretches.

My timidity was obvious. It invited people to take advantage of me. To this day I remain afraid to swim or drive or to do anything that might pose the risk of harm. I became paranoid and constantly felt I was swimming against the tide in day-to-day situations. I found it increasingly hard to relax and go with the flow—often obsessing about what bad thing might happen next.

My father saw the changes in me, and they made him go inward. Increasingly, he regretted never taking us to the UK earlier, blaming

himself for the horrors of everyday life, even things beyond his control. That was unfair to him. His health restricted our movements, not to mention the family's acute lack of resources. My parents had long resigned themselves to a destiny of dying in India, but they never lost hope their children might find a happier existence elsewhere.

It was a confusing time. I was too young to grasp fully the range of emotions inside me, especially as I dealt with bullying and harassment. I do remember being angry, which both then and looking back now seemed warranted. The risk was my anger transforming into hate. My parents, particularly my mother, were vigilant in teaching us about the power of love and that we should reject hatred out of hand. They wanted us to understand why people did mean things and, while easier said than done, to feel empathetic towards them, even when they directed their meanness at us. Despite what I'd learned from my parents and, not the least, Donna, it took an extraordinary turn of events for me to comprehend and embrace the profound powers of compassion and forgiveness.

Because I had previously returned to school after a long hiatus and performed well, my mother assumed I could readily make up for missed studies. So, she again had me do a stint at home to help out. This morphed into a pattern that lasted several years. I enjoyed being a child that got to feel like a mother. It boosted my confidence, which I sorely needed, and made me see myself stronger than perhaps I was. I'd come home to look out for the children for a while, return to school, come home again for months, and so on.

Being home allowed me to do other things besides caretaking at home. Ever since I was nine or ten, I had an interest in caring for the elderly and so, during one home installment, I decided to spend time at assisted homes that cared for our most frail and needy seniors. And I roped Vanessa into working with me. As often as we could, we'd queue up for rations and clothes at the Sisters of Charity centers and haul our bounty to the elderly. It became a routine and a passion.

Sometimes Vanessa and I saved and used our modest pocket money, perhaps one or two rupees, to buy biscuits, bread, medicine, and, if we had enough, jam, as gifts for our elders.

Our primary motive was giving to those elderly who had little or nothing. We delighted in sharing what few gifts we managed to put together. It was the weekly highlight to show up at the facility to find them eagerly on the lookout for us. Many weren't blessed with visitors and I kept a special place in my heart for them. Once we arrived, we made the rounds, placing a slice of bread on each of their laps before spreading a spoonful of jam over the top. They loved it.

Then, one day, there was an unexpected and jolting twist. We learned that Mrs. Green—the worst abuser of my life—lived there. I instantly froze with anxiety.

In the normal course of our work at the home, we would care for her. But given the horror of our history together, how could I? Should I even try? Vanessa cautioned me to leave her alone, to put my attention and efforts elsewhere, concerned she might still be cruel or that seeing her might unnerve or send me into a bad place. I insisted on seeing her. We were at the home to help everyone within our capacity to help. It was not for us to discriminate among any of the needy. For sure, I was incredibly nervous; I shook as I ambled towards where she was sitting. I wondered how she'd react when she saw me, what she might say or recall. I wondered how I would handle the moment we saw each other. But when I saw Mrs. Green, sitting in her chair, looking innocent and unawares, I was overcome with empathy and heartfelt concern. She was withered and frail and seemed mentally disconnected from the world. She did not remember either of us. She was suffering from dementia and was in a bad way. She needed love and attention, and I wasn't going to deny her that.

The more time we spent with her, the greater sympathy for her plight blossomed in our hearts, to the point where eventually, we could honestly say, we loved her. And once we could appreciate that,

behind the cruelty and beatings, she had her own demons from her past to overcome and, despite the crosses *she* had to bear, she was one of a few who extended a helping hand to our family, we also felt grateful to her.

We spent considerable time with her and never once felt the slightest bit of hatred. We danced about and adored her, taking care of her as we did the others. We read to her, wiped her down, hugged her, combed her hair, and kissed her. It might seem strange, but the bad memories melted away and were a total non-factor in how we treated her. Nothing from those terrible times took away the love and gratitude we felt for her.

As I look back, there's no doubt Mrs. Green took some of her frustrations out on us—I'll never forget that wretched toilet—but she touched my sister and me in myriad small ways. If nothing else, I will remain forever grateful that she relieved some of the stress my mother felt about having to fend for us on her own and the worrying about our precarious family situation.

I'm sure she must have done some good in her life, but I was also convinced she had suffered. Our visits and kindness, when nobody else wanted her, brought her joy. Sometimes she used to hold our hands and fall asleep. We'd stay perfectly still to not disturb her. I don't know what she felt or was thinking—or if she ever recognized us—but to have the opportunity, before she died, to thank her for everything she did meant the world to us.

The experience with Mrs. Green, in spite of my relatively young age, opened my eyes wide to what my mother meant when she often spoke about the vital importance of empathy. To interact with Mrs. Green the way we did, to have compassion for her despite how badly she abused me, and get free of the associated pain, elevated me to a new spiritual plane. Equally profound, it placed me more assuredly on a life course that would define and sustain me.

17 | A Girl Like Me

I arrived at an age where a boyfriend was the social norm, except for the stigma that Anglo-Indian poor girls like me were socially "untouchable." In other words, unworthy of such frolicking happiness. Inside the universe of my social world, romantic relationships were fraught with bitter disappointment. For some Anglo-Indian girls, the objects of their affection abruptly disappeared without a clue or word. Here one day, gone the next—literally. Others followed down primrose paths to marriage only to get summarily tossed aside as the happy day approached. *Sorry, can't do this.* Some men duped my friends into parting with sizeable amounts of money before they vanished. In other more heart-wrenching situations, men fell in love with an Anglo-Indian girl, lived and had children with them, and then bolted, abandoning the family.

All suffered not merely the pangs of rejection—for that happens— but bouts of feeling indelibly unworthy because of their cultural identity. In virtually all the cases, families of the men would not permit them to spend time with or marry girls from our community. The pressure of disapproval stayed constant. We were forbidden fruit,

good enough to sample out of taboo curiosity but not good enough to keep. So, we often got discarded on a whim.

Across from my all-girls school sat an all-boys school. As might be expected of a boarding school rooted in British tradition, intermingling was frowned upon but equally expected in the natural order of things; the genders gravitated to each other, mingled, and got acquainted. I was no exception. When fourteen, I dropped some books while walking, and before I could retrieve them, an Indian boy rushed over to pick them up. How gallant I thought. We started talking, one thing led to another, and before long, we were exchanging short missives, characterized by such teenage silliness like, "I like you. Do you like me?"

On my birthday, I received a box with two roses, two cakes, and a letter that contained a formal request for a date. I was thrilled. He had smuggled the box into my dorm with the conspiratorial assistance of a classmate. I got nabbed, however, and because I had violated the no-fraternizing rule, the school confiscated the gifts. Worse, the school gave me up to my mother the following weekend when she visited, filling her ear with the horrors of my purported social misstep. In a fit of uncharacteristic anger, my mother slapped me, and then, much to my chagrin, she marched over to the boys school, found the right classroom, and, in front of the whole class, slapped my erstwhile boyfriend too.

I assumed at the time that my mother's reaction had less to do with the cultural clash than entering the no-fraternization zone. Still, it was a rare moment when my mother disappointed me. I thought I deserved more understanding and compassion in the circumstances.

It wasn't always that bad. When I was sixteen, with prior parental permission, I began dating another Indian boy. Despite the green

light, my parents worried outwardly that I was getting involved in a relationship that promised no future. But they'd both been teenagers themselves and knew how I was feeling. They cut me some slack.

The object of my affection was a polite boy named Sushil who hailed from a wealthy family. His father ran multiple oil businesses. We got on well, but as night follows day, the cultural taboos reared their head, and not in subtle ways. We'd exit school and begin to walk down the road together, but the moment he saw anyone who might know him, he'd cross the street, leaving me alone. His explanation was unambiguous and frank: he couldn't be seen with me. It hurt. But being young, I thought I was in love. I shoved the slight aside.

I pressed my parents to allow a home visit. I'd seen his home—from the outside—a relative palace with marble floors and endless windows that compared starkly with our veranda with no door and a plastic curtain. But I was proud of the relationship and keen to show him off to my parents. After give and take, they agreed to let him visit on Christmas Day. The day started off on the wrong foot.

That morning I had sported a new dress to church. It was made of material that looked like newsprint with a blushing pink background, a fashionable look at the time. I had scrimped and saved pocket money to have it made. I must have ironed the thing for about an hour that morning before we left for church.

The moment we got outside my siblings burst into raucous laughter. Vanessa was pointing to a rickshaw puller who wore a shirt made from the same pink material. I was mortified and wanted to run inside and hide forever. My mother was having none of that—we had to leave for church to make it on time. She made me ride in the same rickshaw. On the way, we passed friends, each gleefully pointing out the matching clothes. I wanted to bury myself in a hole.

I eagerly looked forward to erasing the morning humiliation when my boyfriend visited that evening. He was tall and had to bend way down to lift up the curtain and come into our little room, but

he displayed no airs. He showed respect. The room contained only two small tables, a single bed, and a tin box where people could sit rather than drop to the floor. We also had a rusted old folding chair my father occupied in a corner. My boyfriend sat on the bed. I tried my best to be demure as my father asked him questions. Holding a glass of orange juice, my boyfriend was in mid-sentence when we heard a "thud," and next thing we saw, the poor boy was folded in two in a V-shape, orange juice in hand, long legs up in the air. He was stuck and stunned. The wooden batons that ran under the bed had snapped and he had fallen onto another tin box my mother had inserted to hold up the batons.

Someone had donated the bed to us. The batons were mostly in poor condition. The mattress was thin: a few lumps of misshapen cotton covered with one of my mother's patchwork quilts. The batons were three inches wide and our mother had used string to tie them together to keep the mattress up.

My mother was matter-of-fact about it, telling everyone not to worry. We only had to pull him out. My younger siblings, however, roared with laughter. I was humiliated, the most embarrassed I'd ever been. I couldn't believe what had happened, the first day my boyfriend visited our home. I burst into tears and wanted to die.

My small-framed mother managed to help him up. She collected the bedding and the broken pieces. There was string and bits of wood and bent tin boxes, including the large one my mother called the coffin. She pulled that out and enlisted the help of my boyfriend to tie up the batons with old string again while my siblings continued their display of hysterics.

After only a short while, he said good night and left. The next day at school, I couldn't bring myself to look at him and went home on my own. It was beyond disgrace. Here I was young and trying to impress, wanting everything to go right. I had cleaned the room from early morning and the long-awaited event culminated in a disaster.

We seemed to get past the visit and continued seeing each other, but the public shunning continued, and it hurt me deeply. Then one day, he announced we couldn't continue because his family would no longer allow him to see (let alone marry) me. I was a Christian, Anglo-Indian girl, an untouchable, and not good enough to be with him. He explained matter-of-factly that was how his parents felt, and it was an off-limits topic between them. He didn't feel as they did but felt helpless to overcome the barrier. He had no say in the matter. And that was that.

I cried bitter tears when I got home. I told my father the news. He knew from prior private discussions about the public shunning. I'd ask if there was some problem with me. He'd always say without hesitation there wasn't and would lift me up. This time he sat me down and teed up one of his favorite Dolly Parton songs, *Chicken Every Sunday*, where Parton sings about how her mother told her she was just as good as any guy out there.

"I know I've played this before," he said as he got out the cassette player, "but let's listen to it one more time."

"Why does he get so upset to be seen with me?" I'd asked.

"I could give you a whole range of reasons why they cannot be seen with us and why they think of us like this but listen to this song," he'd said. "Dolly talks about how people didn't want to be seen with her and how her mother used to tell her that just because they have got that big old house on the hill, he thinks he is better than her but he is not better, she is just as good as him. The same goes for you Jillu. You are better than him, and you're better off without him." I loved that song and every word meant the world to me. It gave me the confidence and the strength to go on at a time when I felt literally worthless.

Despite all I'd been through, life lessons still held the capacity to shock me. I was amazed how, without bothering to get to know you, people easily judged; that regardless of your values, accomplishments,

and reputation, people were quick to condemn you. How can that be right or fair, I'd ask myself. How can someone cast us aside as untouchables without knowing us, other than superficially, simply because we were different in origin?

It was worse with my boyfriend who knew my qualities and nonetheless recoiled from public association, fearing someone might betray him to his family for his forbidden behavior. I understood the dire consequences he faced that might taint his future. He too was a victim, for no "decent" Indian family would allow their daughter to marry him if he had been with an Anglo-Indian girl. He showered me with compliments, about how good I was and about my heart of gold. But he couldn't overcome the fright his family had instilled in him. He could not come to terms with facing up to them.

But amid the bigotry, there were kinder people, those who didn't judge, who showed love and gave respect for who we were. My mother called them the "good souls." They may have been poor and illiterate, but they lived by a strong and simple moral code, with humility and generosity of spirit. They knew implicitly that material possessions didn't mean happiness and for sure didn't assure character. Richness, I was learning, was in how you lived, the actions you took, the way you treated others, and the love you shared.

My father had a saying. "If I left a penny on a table and came back after ten years, I'd expect to find the penny where I'd left it." He expected honesty.

As Paulo Coelho put it, "the world is changed by your example, not by your opinion."

I am a proud Anglo-Indian. I am proud of my ancestry and the work my community has done and continues to do selflessly in India. We are a body of people who loves and helps others in need unconditionally, without knowing or judging them. I'm proud to be "a girl like me."

18 | Moving to Delhi

Once I finished school in 1988, my father wanted me to leave the area to avoid increased risks of sexual abuse. We went by train to my elder sister's house in Delhi. Things didn't work there for multiple reasons. I then moved to my other sister Barbara's house, also in Delhi. Meanwhile, Vanessa enrolled in a teaching program in the city of Pune, almost 1,500 kilometers south of Delhi. The little ones were now enrolled in St. Thomas' boarding school.

When I reached Delhi, Barbara did all she could for me, but she was getting on her feet herself after relocating from Bombay. She had no means to look after me or pay for my further education. I stayed with her for a short while before moving in with a couple who were family friends. They graciously paid for a secretarial course and much of my subsistence and looked after me like one of their own. I was lucky to live with them. For the first time in my life, I was able to experience a sense of stability. While they never said so, it was clear they were willing to have me stay permanently. I am forever grateful to them and have tried in every way to repay the debt.

Their kindness helped me acquire essential qualifications, which got me an interview for a secretarial position with ALM International, an export company in the suburbs that provided professional manpower to the Middle East. I was so anxious at the interview, I kept making mistakes, filling the bin with paper as I made typing errors. I couldn't stop crying during the test but somehow managed to stay focused, get the job, and for the first time, join the working-class ranks.

My bright, new, promising path, however, didn't allow me to leave the immense struggles of Calcutta life behind. To get to work, I had to endure a long bus ride—a daily journey I'll never forget. The bus had a capacity of less than fifty and normally transported one hundred. It had two sets of doors where people assembled disproportionately. I boarded near the start of the route, which allowed me to grab a seat in the front and exit with relative ease, without pushing through a packed assembly of lecherous men groping me.

Most days I'd see the same woman sitting at the first window seat and do my utmost to sit beside her to eliminate the chance of sitting next to a man and lower the risk of a physical advance. It was a strategy that didn't always work. Sitting on the aisle seat still allowed men to rub their groins into my shoulder, which happened routinely. To counter it, I'd hunch down low into my seat, cry quietly to myself, and pray for my stop quickly to arrive to end the degradation.

My girlfriend who was an Indian girl in the office gave me a safety pin and urged me to use it, but I could never summon the gall. I would hold my bag as close as possible to my chest as a buffer. I couldn't even look up without a man being right there, making inappropriate gestures and advances.

The second the lady next to me rose to leave the bus men descended to compete for the seat, scooting across my lap. Some, incredibly, tried to climb through the window, feet first, to sit near me, leaving mud and dirt on my clothes. Once there, they'd start

the rubbing and touching without a word as if it were inadvertent. I dreaded the process of going to work. Gearing up to face a blitz of mistreatment and seeing faces stare at me as I boarded the bus is something no girl should have to face.

I was, of course, happy to join the company that employed me. I wanted to earn enough money to live and help my parents. It was a family business, which normally would have been fine, except the son and nephew of the owner constantly pressured me to go out with them. When I refused, they made me work late, which took me out of the local transportation schedule. It was too dangerous to walk to the bus stop alone. The nearest stop was three miles away, the surrounding area under development, pitch-black without streetlights, with no women around: nothing but piles of sand, cement, and building materials, and hundreds of men lurking about on the roadside. I'd rather have slept at work than venture to the bus stop on my own at night.

Knowing this, the two would offer me a ride home in their cars. They knew it was the only viable choice and naturally I'd accept. Most often the ride home was unbearable. I'd have to play games to avoid sexual contact beyond the groping. In desperation, I befriended a man at work who agreed to pick me up after work and drop me home. It kept the others at bay and got me home safely and unmolested. We got close in the natural course of events.

Then I discovered he was married with five children and a wife who never left the house. Others at work threatened to expose him. Again, learning the hard way, I cut him off, which was considerably less bothersome than facing again the challenge of getting home after work on my own. What hurt even more was learning later that he saw me as an opportunity to have sex with a "foreign" girl. Thankfully, that never happened.

The ordeal exhausted me. I felt alone and confused and distrustful. I worried about losing my job. I also didn't know how I'd get home at

night safely if I continued working late. I did emerge with my dignity intact, which counted for a lot. But on balance, I knew I had to find another job. After several months, I found a new temporary, but better paying, position with Rohde & Schwartz, a German manufacturer of aerospace equipment. The extra pay freed me to send money home regularly. I moved into a small room of my own a considerable distance from where I had to report to work. I was moving forward in increments. I felt twinges of freedom coming on.

As I continued searching for something permanent, I received devastating news.

19 | A Noble Fighter

Longevity doesn't include overtime credit for suffering. Sustained sorrow and unwavering personal sacrifice and neglect over the course of a life can extract a steep price for anyone to pay, no matter how good-natured their intentions or much love is shared. There is only so much the mind, spirit, and body can bear. Eventually, something—or everything—has to give.

The body is the telltale. It is a machine and requires care. When it doesn't get the attention it needs, it breaks down, often in the form of terminal illness. The worst is never over. It has its own timetable. Too many years of not eating so others could, seeking to kill hunger with copious amounts of black tea, smoking cheap cigarettes habitually, and shouldering inconceivable emotional stress, is not a life-sustaining formula.

And so, sad as it was, it was not surprising that after a visit to the doctor, my mother received the news she had cervical cancer.

The signs had been there. She had begun looking haggard, and each day she seemed more physically and mentally exhausted. Her concentration had wavered and she sometimes seemed disconnected

from reality. She had endured too much for too long, and I could see futility in her eyes—she was grappling with whether she could or should go on much longer. The will to live was slipping from her. She had kept up the good fight of late because she had two little ones to care for, but they were now away in school. She finally had to face the realities she had managed to brush off. Giving up so much for her children, those she loved the most, had crushed her.

Her decline came swiftly, each day more difficult to manage. My father wrote me with this ominous message: "If you and your sisters wish to see your mother alive in the next few months, you will need to take her to Delhi for treatment. Otherwise, we'll lose her soon."

We had no one in Kidderpore to care for her. My father worked long days to pay the bills, support himself, and keep the little ones in school. Vanessa and I had moved away and my older siblings had their own families—and problems—to handle. They struggled to make ends meet and lacked the bandwidth to care for anyone else, especially someone terminally ill.

My mother never expressed disappointment in the older siblings. She knew their thoughts were with her, but they couldn't help her. She knew they did the best they could with the resources they had. Special as she was, my mother did not feel let down. She knew they each loved her dearly.

The news of my mother's illness of course unsettled me. In the first instance, I wasn't quite sure how to deal with it. I didn't feel grounded enough to seize the moment. While I had begun to develop some sense of who I was, the truth was, I wasn't entirely sure. I lacked direction and didn't have a life vision or a path. But with some emotional dust settling, I figured out this much: my mother, who gave me and the family her best, needed me. The tables had turned. It was my turn to look after her. I wasn't the eldest but I was her child, and I understood my role.

I arranged to bring her to Safdarjung, a free hospital in Delhi, in hopes of better medical treatment. When she arrived, her eyes spoke what her broken heart couldn't express in spoken words: enough was enough. She was reduced to taut skin and bone. She looked resigned. We clung to hope. We assumed she'd be better off there than in Calcutta. We assumed wrong. The hospital conditions were as dire as in Calcutta. The hospital was chaotic, filthy, and a horrible place. But with no disposable funds, we had no alternative but to find her a free hospital. Each day hundreds of poor people lined up for a blood test or a scan. Like ants going to and from a nest, would-be patients and their families streamed in and out of the hospital. Most came from slums or nearby villages. Most were destitute people who didn't know where to go or how to navigate the hospital system to get medical assistance.

The hospital where my mum was admitted

Registration alone took a few days. Rules required that new patients be present for the entire registration process so the clerk could eyeball them. Long unruly queues were overflowing with ailing patients, many too sick to know where they were and some in agonizing pain, screaming, and moaning. You needed a different kind of resilience to see the process through. My mother and I waited, and waited, and stayed the course. It was a nightmare.

I got her admitted and, after weeks of struggle and persistence, the hospital arranged for surgery, followed by radiotherapy. She was hospitalized for seven months. I visited her each morning before work to clean, feed, and sit with her. I returned in the evening after work.

I had a new boyfriend at the time, Shane, an Anglo-Indian boy, who gave me unconditional support. Shane was a wholly decent person with a heart of gold and an inner strength and humility most don't possess. When I had to bring my brother Neil to Delhi because my father was too old to care for him, Shane cared for him. There were no questions asked, nothing expected in return, and not a care about himself.

Shane also helped out at our home during this period. And, to ease my journey a little, he joined me when he could and helped with my mother. He helped me bathe, dress, and feed her, and did whatever he could to make life better for her. I shall be forever grateful for his kind heart. He was essential to my getting through this.

The process took a toll on me. I was traipsing back and forth between the hospital, the place I worked, and home. I traveled on countless buses, so crowded I often sat on the floorboards, collapsed in exhaustion.

The hospital atmosphere didn't help. On the contrary, it beat me down. It was a depressing and demoralizing place. Sick people were scattered everywhere, sitting in corridors, passageways, down the aisles, and in the main reception area, day and night. The place reeked of vomit, urine, excreta, and disinfectants so powerful the

scent penetrated the air outside the hospital. People constantly cried out in pain, hunched on the floor, holding their stomachs, their backs, and their heads. Women cried and screamed. Some bashed their heads against walls after loved ones passed away. Children relieved themselves behind pillars or on old newspaper. Aged people, unable to stand, folded in a heap to the floor. People fought over strewn scraps of food and dirty linen. People in need were left lying unattended on stretchers. Others lay there dead.

Sometimes there were student protests against the government, who were at the time supporting scheduled castes and scheduled tribes. The protests blocked routes to the hospital. Bombs went off. Riot police dispersed tear gas. Students set themselves on fire. Lengthy processions spread for miles. The police, outnumbered by at least a thousand, suffered violence.

Each day, however, I managed to penetrate the walls of chaos to see my mother and bring her a juice or something to eat. I never strayed from my mission. I never lost hope. I never entertained for a second not being there for her or trying to save her life with every ounce of me.

Months in, I was close to complete collapse and at a breaking point. I feared I might not be able to cope much longer. I kept reminding myself of my commitment to keep my mother alive.

Then the dark clouds separated slightly and a slice of manna dropped. I ran into a medical student named Dr. Sandeep Uppal, an Indian boy who, as it turned out, once took drum lessons from my brother-in-law. Sandeep was doing his residency at the hospital. He had pledged his life to help others in one of the harshest medical environments on Earth.

Sandeep went out of his way to make life easier for us at that hospital. He couldn't cure my mother, but he soothed our way forward. If it weren't for him, I don't see how I'd have carried on as long as I did. He had a heart of pure gold. He loved my mother like his own and made personal sacrifices to help her. He was a lifeline.

In my experience, it is rare to find a doctor with so much compassion or encounter a younger person with so much love in his heart and devotion to people in need. I marveled as I watched him routinely stop and talk to people, lend them a hand, show them the way, give them advice, and do about anything to help them. He toiled tirelessly throughout the day while other doctors seemed overwhelmed, often not even stopping to answer questions. Sandeep put aside caste, creed, religion, color, and race. He only saw fellow human beings. He inspired me, and my family owes him much gratitude. It is said people come into your life for a reason. There is no better illustration of this than Sandeep.

My mother eventually left the hospital. She was still suffering. She was still hanging on.

20 | Saying Goodbye

My mother insisted on coming home. She fell prey to worries about my father and the children who were still in Calcutta. We obliged, but once home, her condition quickly worsened. Susan, only twelve years old at the time, came home from school to administer to her. Susan was aware that Mum was terminally ill, but she did not know the brutal truth that she was suffering from metastatic cancer. She would rub our mother's back and arms for hours, using a pain relief ointment and dipping a dirty rag in lukewarm water to make a compress. Her care was virtually 24/7.

It was sad beyond belief. We were ill-equipped to care for her. The situation needed to change; we needed professional help. I had no choice but to take my mother back to Delhi. We tried to go back to the Safdarjung Hospital for more radiation therapy, but they were at capacity and wouldn't admit her. We eventually found another free hospital, the Lok Nayak Jai Prakash Narayan Hospital (LMJP), which had an available bed. The doctors placed Mum in a general ward among thirty patient-filled beds. The stench was unbearable, the atmosphere chaotic and rampant with screaming and anguish. It

was a futile exercise. She could no longer walk on her own and grew weaker by the day no matter what the doctors did. I hated acting as if hope would suddenly spring when we had every reason to know otherwise. To make matters worse, Daddy couldn't visit the hospital because he lacked the means. It was a low point for our family.

I took an advance on all my benefits and annual salary from Rohde & Schwarz to buy Mum's medicines, food, and other nourishment, but it was never enough, and I was left with no money to pay my rent and other bills. I approached my sister Barbara for help finding a second job. She located a nighttime job as a singer in a hotel. She knew the lead guitarist and he said he'd help out. I couldn't sing a lick; I took the job anyway.

I had a new routine: I worked during the day in office clothes, then after work, I'd meet my boyfriend at a nearby bus stop to retrieve a second-hand cocktail dress, visit my mum at the hospital, and then hurry to the hotel with just enough time to change my outfit before going on stage, where I remained until 2 a.m. Afterward, I'd go home, rest for two or three hours, rise at 6 a.m., make an early morning hospital visit, and start the pattern all over again.

I never sang. I was far too nervous. I just stood there, thinking about my mother. Eusdon, the guitarist, told me not to worry. He said all they needed was a female presence on stage. Then one day, an irate customer approached the stage. He was a visiting businessman with a strong Punjabi accent.

"She only stands there; she doesn't sing at all!" he bellowed.

"That's right," said Eusdon matter-of-factly, hoping the man would go away.

"But I want to 'ear her. If she don't sing, I'll be complainin' t'management," he retorted, taking out a bundle of notes and slapping them down on the piano.

He returned to his table, grinning to his colleagues. Panic-stricken, I turned to Eusdon.

"Listen, we'll sing *Top of the World*," Eusdon said. "I'll sing with you, but you have to sing because if you don't, they may force me to ask you to leave."

I said I'd do my best, but I was so nervous, the words wouldn't come out. I think I croaked and hummed a little, but I was inaudible. The man demanded his money back and became verbally abusive. Eusdon pushed back hard until he backed off.

"Who cares, Jillian," Eusdon assured me. "Don't worry about it. You are great for us, and you sing like an angel." I almost broke down in tears.

Eusdon shared whatever tips he received, no matter how much. He also gave me a little money to help with my mother's medicine, food, and other needs when he could. His kindness floored me.

I did everything I could to prolong Mum's life. Then a brain scan revealed that the cancer had spread aggressively, including into her spine. The doctor expected the cancer to soon infiltrate the brain and explained that it would be the end.

While on her last trip from Calcutta to Delhi, my mother fractured her right collar bone and arm. The radiation and chemotherapy had likely made her bones brittle. One of the doctors also explained that it was not uncommon for tumors to grow to a size capable of breaking bones, especially in metastatic cases like Mum's. The doctors kept putting off a date to set the injury in plaster. Mum kept asking, and they kept delaying. We were all confused, and the waiting felt like torture. Watching my precious mother in so much pain was hard on all of us. We tried to keep her as comfortable as possible, but our feelings of helplessness were unshakeable.

One night during my usual after-work visit, before I reached my mother's bed, the head surgeon, Dr. Vinay Joshi, pulled me aside, wanting to speak privately.

"I'm sorry, Jillian. Your mother has around fourteen days *at most* to live. You should take her home."

"But there must be something …" I said, my voice trembling.

He shook his head.

"I'm sorry. She's too far gone. There is nothing more we can do."

I didn't reply. I just stood in the doorway of the ward, letting his words hang in the air around me. I must have looked crazed, for the doctor widened his eyes as he tilted his head back.

"Jillian, are you all right?" Dr. Joshi asked.

"Yes, yes, thank you. I'm okay," I replied, snapping out of my trance. He nodded and moved on to his next crisis.

I wanted to burst into tears. But I knew I had to stay strong if only because I could feel my mum staring at us as we talked, eager to hear what the doctor had to say. Despite the doctor's pronouncement, I racked my brain for anything available to reverse the diagnosis. Why had everything I'd done been so ineffective? I struggled to accept the failure of my efforts. What could I have done differently? I walked towards my mother in a daze. I wanted to hold her tightly and cry my heart out. I couldn't understand how life could be so cruel, but there I was, privy to the worst news of my life. I did my best to hide my anguish. It was time for a brave face. Time to be the courageous and dutiful daughter.

"What did the doctor say, Jillu?" Mum asked. I looked into her ravaged face, composed myself with a deep breath, and trained my eyes on her to avoid breaking down.

"I asked if I could take you home for a few days since you've been here a long time. He told me what to do if I took you home tomorrow."

She was excited, and said, "So, come on then … let's go."

I put a hand on her arm. It felt like a twig.

"No, Mum. We have to wait until tomorrow because of paperwork. No staff are available now."

Thankfully, she accepted my story, and so, for the last time in the hospital, I sat with her, and fed and talked to her. I rubbed her back, combed her hair, and kissed her good night. I wanted to stay the night, crawl into her bed, and hold her close to me forever. The thought of leaving her side in that situation was unbearable. Another part of me desperately wanted to find a place to cry my eyes out. Instead, I became robotic, steeling myself, fighting back the flood of tears coming from my heart into my throat. I could sense a breakdown coming on. I wanted a sibling there so I could have someone to cry with. But I was alone. I rose and left the hospital after kissing Mum good night. She held my hand and said, "Jillu, should anything happen to me, promise me that you will take care of the two little ones." I looked at her and said, "Mummy, this is a promise I will never break." In that moment, I felt I had given her permission to let go. Barely two steps out of the ward, I was flooded with loss and grief beyond description.

The certainty of losing her was excruciating, unfathomable. How could this be fair? How could this be real? I felt so alone and vulnerable. Every few steps I had to stop and steady myself. I wanted to curl up in each doorway I passed. I hated that I was incapable of reversing the doctor's words. On the bus, I cried the entire way home, not caring about the stares I was getting. I was in a state of shock, my mind a mix of rational and irrational thoughts. I wanted to believe I'd misheard the doctor or that he was plain wrong, or it was only stress and fatigue catching up with me. I kept trying to escape reality, but it resolutely re-set my mind each time I drifted.

The one thought I couldn't escape was how my mother had such a sad life. She fought through every wretched obstacle thrown into her path and hardly had anything to be happy about, certainly not for a sustained period of time. Life for her had been a continuous struggle. I wanted to take care of her for a little while longer. To make her smile. To make her laugh, even if weakly. I wanted her to enjoy

one breath after the other; I wanted her to not stop breathing. To this day, I do not know how I got home or how the rest of the night went. It remains a blur.

It was also painful to remind myself that my mother would never fulfill her dream of returning to the UK and reuniting with her siblings. There were two older brothers, Geoffrey and Donald, who emigrated to England soon after Indian Independence. I later discovered that Donald died in Lincolnshire in 1981 and Geoffrey in London in 1995. To the end, Mum harbored the hope of reconnecting, but it was not to be.

The following day, my brother Neil brought our mother home. I made her as comfortable as I could. As futile and irrational as it was, I couldn't give up on trying to save her. I resumed nursing her, refusing to accept what the doctor had said. I thought we could nurse her back to health if we just tried hard enough. I was in deep denial, banking on a miracle. She kept asking why the doctors hadn't scheduled a procedure to set her collar bone and her arm, wondering if it was because she was dying. I told her no, they were worried that the anesthetic might react with the strong medications she was on. They wanted her condition to improve before setting the bones. She seemed pleased with that answer. The pain she had from the cancer, by comparison, dwarfed the pain in her arm. The doctor also told me that the morphine she was taking probably eliminated any pain from the broken bones. At least that was one small relief.

Her condition worsened by the day. I had to feed her with liquids. I stayed up with her virtually all night, but within a week, she had slipped into a coma. I finally had to accept that she would never wake up.

It was time to think of next steps. One of the hardest things I've ever faced was borrowing money for a coffin and making funeral arrangements before she'd even passed. The doctor told me that in her condition, we shouldn't attempt to keep the body. Yet, a desperate

part of me still felt she might wake up and feel better at any moment. My elder siblings were busy with their own lives and families and I didn't want to burden my younger siblings or my father, so I felt I had no one to share my innermost feelings with.

I hated myself for ordering her coffin and preparing her burial while she was still alive. I loved her more than ever but lived every day in turmoil trying to do what I had to. On top of making the arrangements in Delhi, it was also up to me to keep my father in Calcutta informed. We discussed what we should tell Susan and Neil, how to handle the hospital expenses, and the weight of trying to maintain our full-time jobs through our sorrow. All the while I couldn't stop blaming myself for failing my mother.

By then, I was almost poverty-stricken myself. I wasn't receiving income because of the advances I'd taken. Scratching out an existence, I took on more and more debt to keep us afloat. We lived in a small room with a bed and a metal closet and nothing more. Every moment and every penny went towards caring for my mother and little brother and sending my father some money whenever I could. Concerned about the age and health of my father, I wondered how I could take Susan off his hands and care for her myself.

On September 13, 1993, I awoke at 5:50 a.m. to check on my mother. She was still breathing. I tidied her hair and patted her with a cool, wet towel before lying down on the floor at her bedside. I fell into a sleepy daze. Shane was in a deep sleep on the floor from pure exhaustion.

Shortly after 6 a.m., I felt as if the entire world had come to a silent halt. Usually, we heard vendors shouting out, people filling water and scuttling to and fro, and children squealing and hollering. A hush replaced the normal sounds, blanketing the world around us, as if to let her pass in peace. I heard nothing except my beating heart. It was a deathly silence. I rose to look at my mother. She seemed peaceful. Her breathing had stopped. She was gone.

I sat with her for a long time, telling her, "I know that you are still here, and you know how much I love you and how grateful I am to you. Please stay with me and help me look after the little ones. I promise never to leave them." I kissed her, thinking what a strong woman I'd had as a mother and how honored I was to have the opportunity to spend those precious moments alone with her. I didn't want to wake anyone. I wanted to sit with her forever. There was still so much I wanted to tell her, so much I wanted to do for her.

Eventually, I woke Shane and told him she had passed and that I needed to go and inform family members. One of the saddest memories I have is running through the streets on my messenger mission, continuously sobbing and struggling to breathe, consumed with sadness and a sense of desperation, oblivious to the world around me. Finally arriving at my first stop, I knocked on the door where family lived, and when they appeared, I blurted out "Mummy is dead, please come." One of them said, "You've given the message, now f**k off!" I was shattered. I could hardly believe my ears. If ever there was a time when family could hurt you the most, when their compassion mattered the most, it was in that moment.

I left, ran down the steps, and cried all the way back home.

21 | Lost in the Dark

I informed my father of Mum's passing by getting him to the telephone in a friend's house. He simply said the saddest "thank you" and put the phone down. There was nothing more to be said. Due to his declining health and financial problems, he couldn't make it to her funeral. It saddened me deeply to envision him so alone, overcome with the stark reality that the woman with whom he'd spent so many years, and endured and fought through so much with, was gone, and he couldn't even be with her to pay his respects.

His personal isolation upset me terribly. I knew he was absorbed with grief and I was overwhelmed by the new demands that lay before me, but I could do nothing to change things. There was no money to send him. The seismic shift of my mother's death had left us both adrift, our grief threatening to give way to a deep well of despair.

For at least six months after that dreadful loss, I went to the cemetery every day after work and sat by my mother's grave and cried and talked to her, thanking her for everything and apologizing for not doing more. I was also desperately worried about how I would

manage with two children and no money, especially since I had taken a salary advance for the rest of the year.

How could I go on? I felt shaken to the core, desperately weak, unable to cope; defeat was breathing down my neck. I had lived through unimaginable poverty, helped raise my younger siblings, and watched my little sisters almost die time after time. I had seen my mother work until she dropped, watched her go without food for days on end, and get beaten in my presence, *and* watched my father being openly humiliated by landlords who weren't fit to wipe his shoes. I had survived the relentless trauma of bombs and balloons being thrown at me till I feared my own shadow, experienced rejection, bullying, and unthinkable loss. I had endured punishments not many children would have survived and worked until I didn't have an ounce of strength left in me. But losing my mother was a grief none of these hardships prepared me for.

I wondered why then it was me who was being given such a huge load to carry? The younger ones needed more care than ever now that my mother had passed away, but I felt that I was in no way equipped to deliver this level of care, and quite honestly, I was too young and ill-prepared to take on two children permanently.

I had only recently left Calcutta to try and sort out my own life and now I was being asked to give up on everything to put the little ones first. There was a part of me that wanted to give up, to scream from the rooftops, but I couldn't just leave the little ones after all that we had been through. As fragile as I was, I knew I would have to dig deeper than I ever had to find the resilience to do what was being asked of me.

Many questions plagued my mind in the months following her death: Why did my mother have to die so young? Why didn't we have enough money to save her life? Why did my younger siblings have to witness so much tragedy? I thought of one of the songs my dad used to play for us, "I Guess That Comes from Being Poor,"

but that did little to comfort me and I found myself bitterly angry with God.

How could God take my mother after I gave everything of myself to get her well? Didn't she, as such a loving, caring, and selfless soul, deserve some time in happiness and relief from worrying about herself and others? While watching her children benefit from her efforts made her happy, it came at a terrible cost to herself. Despite my anger and feelings of hopelessness, I couldn't find a reason to walk away from the little ones or abandon my responsibilities. I reflected on my parents' lives, their hardships, and tried desperately to think of what they would do in my situation.

My father was a boxer when he was young, and I remember him saying that if there was one lesson he had learned it was to find the resilience to stand up every time he got knocked down. The blows themselves didn't matter; the toughest job of all was finding the strength to stand up again when you were down on the floor, ready to give up. If you could do that, the crowds would then motivate you to go on. It is the same when a person is taught to get back on a horse right away after they have fallen off. The idea is to train the mind to bury that fear at the appropriate time and prove to *yourself* that you are better than that punch or that fall or that situation.

He told us that there would be times in life when we would be down on the floor, with an opponent looking over our heads waiting for us to stay down in defeat, but it is at that point that we need to remember that we are only down, but not out, and if we can find the strength to stand up again, one last time, we can find our way back to try all over again.

I had heard the story many times, but this time the message finally sunk in, under my skin and into my bones: the moment you refuse to accept your situation and commit to fighting back, the magic begins. But my confidence in myself was still quite shaky and I wondered if I was capable of such perseverance.

With everything that had happened to me, I had always felt defective in some way. I was not like my other siblings; I was fearful and jumpy, and my sisters often called me a wimp. I couldn't shake the feeling that Mrs. Green was probably right to tell my mother that I would never be good at anything. Lucky for me, my father always had a story ready for every problem that we put to him and I recalled him telling me a story that he had read while he was recovering from a heart attack at the Salvation Army about an old lady and a bucket.

> An old woman had two buckets which she used to fetch water from a river some distance away from her home. One of these buckets had a small hole that always leaked water as the woman walked home. The other bucket was intact and held the water well. By the time the woman returned home, almost half of the water in the first bucket had leaked away through the hole.
>
> One day something strange happened; the defective bucket felt bad for its imperfection and spoke to the old woman. It apologized for always wasting almost half of the water and not being as relevant and useful as the other bucket. "I understand if there is a need to replace me with a better bucket." The old woman smiled and asked the bucket, "You think I don't know about the hole? See all the flowers that I planted along the course to the river? They have always been watered by you because the water leaks through that tiny hole you have." The bucket never knew that its imperfection was the actual source of its relevance.

Then he had reminded me of how my mother used to take the oldest of rags and sew them together to create the most beautiful coats, quilts, and household ornaments that one could only marvel at. This reminded me of the quote by Dr. Wayne Dyer, "If you change

the way you look at things, the things you look at change." In my darkest hour, I reflected on these stories, and I could literally feel my father speaking to me. I knew that my parents would have wanted me to believe in myself and to take what I had and turn it into something extraordinary. That would be the biggest gift I could give them.

Thinking about my mother reminded me of something from my teenage years and it made me smile. My mother brought many people home from the streets to stay with us over the years, but the one I recall most was Errol. He was dirty and scruffy when she brought him home, and after she got him cleaned up and dressed in my father's old clothes, she sent him out to shop for tomatoes and potatoes from the nearby vendors to make the bottled soup she brought to Vanessa and me at school. While he was out, I came home and decided to take a bath, which consisted of squatting on the veranda and scooping water from a plastic bucket.

As I mentioned before, the veranda didn't have a door—only a plastic curtain and an old blanket as a roof to stop the men upstairs from looking down on us. I was washing myself when Errol lifted up the curtain and walked straight in, giving me a huge grin. I screamed and burst into tears.

"What's wrong with you?" my mother asked, rushing out onto the veranda.

"He can't just walk in like that because I am a girl and I am having a bath!"

"If we had a door, he would have knocked, but we don't have a door, so what do you expect him to do?" she snapped.

"But Mum, the veranda has the plastic curtain, but the room has a door."

"But he can't get to the door, so what do you expect him to do? Fly over the blanket? He has to get onto the veranda to get to the door of the room, so he has to come in that way. Do you want him to walk through the wall?"

"But Mum, I'm a girl and you know I'm growing up and—"

"Now just you listen Jillian Haslam. When you become Elizabeth Taylor and start looking like her then come talk to me, other than that, grow up, and stop thinking too much of yourself. There is nothing you have that he hasn't seen before. He has sisters, he has a mother, he has seen everything—so get over it! Put on your clothes and get cracking."

That was how she was. She never let anyone yield to their emotions or take themselves too seriously. She always focused on moving forward, no matter what. As I thought more about how I needed to change my situation, I imagined her standing before me, telling me to get on with what I needed to do and to stop thinking too much of myself. She would not waste any time on being sad when others were depending on her. I decided I had to be more like my indomitable mother.

My mother often told us never to allow negativity, misfortune, or bitterness to find homes in our hearts and as I thought of how strong my parents were and that all they ever wanted was for us to love each other, stick together, and look out for each other, I knew just what I had to do.

I made my peace with God, accepting that things always happen for a reason and that He helps those who seek to help themselves. I promised myself I would do what my mother wanted—to care for the two young ones as my mother had. I would also get my father to Delhi as soon as possible and look after him too. I knew my mother would want that as well. In death, she had become my beacon.

22 | A Foot on the Ladder

While my grieving continued, I also began to feel twinges of hope—not merely in moving forward, emotionally intact, but in how I could be of service to others. I didn't have a clear vision, or any game plan, but I had a rough and slowly developing sense of wanting to honor my parents through deeds of kindness. Even when they had next to nothing, they never stopped thinking of other people. Especially my mother, not only when it came to her own children, but all who struggled to make it through the day, whose plights were as bad or worse than ours. She naturally put herself second, an engrained mindset that transcended self-interest. Knowing who she was allowed me to refocus myself, for the time being, on my younger siblings, Neil and Susan. My mission would begin there. It empowered me.

All of the lessons we had been taught proved prophetic when I received an invitation from an employment agency to apply for a job with American Express. This was an opportunity that could change all of our lives and I knew I must go for it. While initially uplifted by the offer to apply, I came back to Earth after learning

that more than sixty women were competing for the post, almost all of them more qualified than I was. Still, I knew I owed it to my mother, and my siblings who were now counting on me, to give it my best effort.

Incredibly, I survived several months and rounds of tests and evaluations and qualified for an interview with my possible boss. My life story struck a chord with him, and he offered me the job. He explained that my sincerity and strong sense of honesty clinched it for him. I was elated. His affirmation gave me confidence that I could discharge my responsibilities effectively. Better, it heralded an improved life.

The job allowed Shane, the two little ones, and me to move to better accommodations, big enough for my father to join us later. For the first time, happiness edged towards the norm. We would soon be able to leave sorrow behind us.

After a year, I was working out of a five-star hotel suite. Each day, I noticed a young boy, perhaps five years old, carrying crates of Coca-Cola bottles on his back. One morning I stopped him.

"What's your name?" I asked.

"Santosh, madam," he replied.

"My name's Jillian … not madam." I smiled.

"Yes, madam," he said and grinned, his face lighting up. I smiled back.

"Who makes you carry those heavy crates around? It's crazy."

"My brother. It's the only way we can get money."

"What about your parents?"

He looked down at the floor before sitting sullenly on his crate.

"They are in Nepal. We have no money. My brothers and me, we come here to make money."

In that moment, I called up the photograph of my mother I kept on my desk and something inside me stirred.

"Well, you tell your brother I want to see him."

"Why?"

"You'll see."

His older brother, who looked about sixteen, turned up the next day to meet with me in the business suite. I asked about their parents. He told me their father had died and their mother lived in Nepal. They never expected to see each other again. Their mother felt that the boys had a better chance of surviving in India and she did not want to leave Nepal.

"I see. And so you have to be a parent to Santosh?"

"I do what I can," he replied, looking at the floor. "We have two other brothers but they are older than Santosh."

"What if I was to help?" I asked. He looked up and furrowed his brow.

I felt inspired to carry on my mother's legacy of helping anyone in need. I told the brother I'd like to "adopt" Santosh and give him a home.

His eyes immediately brightened, as if I'd offered him untold amounts of money. Then, his eyes narrowed and he looked wary.

"Why?" He asked suspiciously.

"Because there is something about him, his character. The goodness in him stands out like a beacon. It deserves to be kept bright. Do you understand what I'm saying?" He nodded and looked around the room as if searching for something to say.

"He is good. He never complains and is always honest. One day, he saw someone drop some money and he ran after them to give it back. Anyone else would have … So, you saw that in him?"

"I did. So, what do you think?"

"I think it would be amazing," he said, flashing the same grin his brother had the day before.

So, with his mom's blessing—"Please, you'll be doing us a great favor"—I made the proper arrangements, took Santosh home, and began to raise him with Neil and Susan. I stayed in touch with his mother and brother, and today, Santosh is as close to me as a brother can be and is a top DJ in Delhi.

Life continued apace. Two years later, my boss returned to the US. I was sad to see him go and worried for my job. I assumed his successor would choose their own Executive Assistant. At the same time, a similar role working for the CEO of Bank of America was being advertised in all the newspapers. It paid much more and would be a major step up. I once again pushed aside my fears and applied.

I was thrilled when I got called for an interview. When I arrived, however, my heart sank. I was competing with two hundred and fifty girls. I took a seat in a huge hall and completed the requisite paperwork and tests. Scanning the area, I shuddered and quickly reminded myself of the promise I'd made to my mother to take care of the younger ones. I *had* to get this job.

I received several callbacks, going through months of tests and interviews with other managers. Each time the applicant pool narrowed, bringing me closer to the opportunity. Eventually, three of us remained. I was both excited to have made it that far—one step closer to my dream, and harbored tremendous anxiety and fear.

The day of the final interview I awoke in a cold sweat, anxious about facing such a man and the magnitude of the job. The scuttlebutt was that he was a demanding character, and it was Bank of America. I was as afraid of succeeding as not. Something I couldn't explain held me back. I tried to convince myself I could handle the job once I had a week or two under my belt, but I couldn't shake the jitters.

I suffered my doubts in silence. My siblings and friends were supportive and encouraging, constantly telling me it was a piece of cake, and they were sure to hire me. But they had no clue what I was really feeling. When we lived in the slums, I had to remain strong and confident for the sake of the little ones. This qualified as one of those times. Outside, I was cool; inside, a bag of nerves.

At the interview, I spoke from my heart. I was as transparent as I could be. I told the CEO I had little ones to support and that even though I might appear shaky, I assured him that if I were given the opportunity and enough time to settle in, I would excel.

I confided to him that sometimes, with significant change, I would get fevers and it might seem like I couldn't cope—like when my mother put me back to boarding school—but in a short while, I'd regain my confidence and rise to any challenge. I told him about the progress prize and how I'd handled two jobs during my mother's illness. I assured him I had what it took to handle the job, stressing that my drive would overshadow any initial concerns. A chance was all I needed.

He listened with a thoughtful look. When I stopped, he continued looking at me for quite a while, and eventually said, "Jillian, you sell yourself in the most honest and remarkable way. I will give this some serious thought and let you know."

I came away worried that I'd said too much. I cursed myself for opening my heart so deeply and going on about my childhood. After all, he was a banker, a hard nut, a person whose operating system likely didn't have room for emotion—someone who could never understand what I had been through or why I was so desperate to succeed. I felt foolish I wasn't more professional and that I allowed myself to appear too eager. I wanted to rewind and start over.

Two weeks later, I answered a knock at the door to see a man handing me an envelope adorned with the BofA logo. I stared at the envelope, turning it over in my hand, fearing that as soon as I opened

it, I'd see the classic rejection words in the first sentence, "We regret to inform you ..."

I was petrified for several minutes. Finally, I took a deep breath and opened the envelope to see an offer of employment. I think I cried for days. Getting the job offer ignited my soul.

But then I learned I'd be replacing the sister of my father's best friend, someone I respected tremendously. She called me on news of the offer.

"Please don't take it," she said.

"What! I've been through months of interviews and waiting and with money like that, I can't afford to not take it."

"He is too much. Over the last few years at least six others have given up—just dropped their pens and literally ran away from the bank. He can be nice, but he's impossible to work with, and he can be unbearable, with virtually no tolerance for mistakes! He throws things and yells, and no time is your own. He is feared by one and all."

"But you lasted," I countered.

"Well, yes. But I'm more resilient, and much, much older than you are."

I pulled my head back. "Don't you think I've had to learn to be like that too?"

She looked at me, nodded, and eked out a small smile.

"Yes, you have, but with all you've been through ..."

I didn't sleep that night. The prospect of working for a man described that way overwhelmed me. No matter what the salary and benefits, I balked at facing a bully each day on the job. I had long had enough of that sort of thing. Besides, I knew myself. I was afraid and timid and not at all prepared to deal with so much so soon.

The next day, I called the head of Human Resources and turned down the offer. I explained I had personal issues to address, and they should give the job to the next best candidate.

The next week he visited me at the house with an envelope.

"I've made up my mind already," I said, handing the envelope back to him.

"Just read it," he said, thrusting it my way once more. "Read it, Jillian."

I tore it open and removed a letter that bore the CEO's letterhead. He had doubled the salary.

"He knows it's not about personal problems. You're the only one he wants."

I have kept both letters with me to this day. They are sacred, reminding me that when something is meant to be, it will.

23 | Bank of America

I'm not sure how I found the nerve, but the first day on the job, in May of 1995, I paraded into my boss's office and told him what I'd heard and said I would not be able to handle that sort of behavior. I couldn't believe the words coming out of my mouth. To up the ante, I added how it might take me a few weeks to settle down and develop the appropriate routines, but I assured him that once I did, he'd never have to worry about my performance, have reason to question my efforts, or find fault with my behavior. I aimed to deliver.

I braced for the blowback. He looked at me—half-seriously, half-amused—didn't say a word, and nodded approvingly. Then, without missing a beat, he assigned my first task. We were off and running! I felt emboldened.

Aware of my weaknesses, I knew that I needed help to grow. From the start, I wanted to embark on a journey to better myself. The first thing I did was locate all of the online training programs that the bank had to offer, and slowly but surely, I went through most of them. I stayed late and went in early; I was hungry to learn and

determined to climb that ladder. I went one step further and asked the CEO if he'd be my mentor.

"No one has ever asked me that before, Jill," he replied, looking a little at a loss.

"I want to know what you know! I'm willing to do anything for an hour of your time, maybe twice a week or even once a week," I said.

He smiled. "Okay, how about this? I have a problem getting my kids to finish their homework. By the time I get home, it's 10 p.m. or so, and they are in bed with half or none of it done. So, if you can help them, I will spend the extra time to help you."

I jumped at the opportunity. For years after, I helped his children with their homework over the phone. In return, he began to change the course of my life. He taught me so much, and along with being my mentor, he became a close friend and my most trusted confidant.

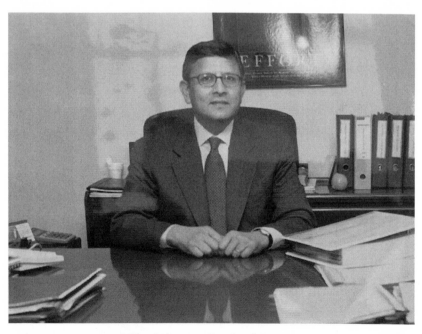

Jillian's boss at Bank of America

I settled in well at Bank of America, and my progress led to another role. My boss got wind of how I tended to hit the streets after work and on weekends to help the poor. He wanted to know why. I explained that I saw my destiny as making a difference in the lives of others by alleviating suffering. He was moved and said he wanted to formalize my efforts.

"I need to change the way things are done here. I'm going to appoint you as President of BofA's Charity and Diversity Network in India."

"You mean you don't want me to work for you anymore?" I asked suddenly panicked that I may have given him the wrong idea about my career aspirations.

"Oh, don't be silly, of course I do. You'll do both jobs, and I'll get you an assistant of your own."

My boss was exceptionally driven. Diligent and hardworking, he expected his staff, especially me, to keep up with his grueling pace. He felt I not only had the capacity to deliver on both roles, but that the charitable program would enhance my performance in the workplace. So he placed me in charge of charitable activities for four metropolitan cities. It was demanding to say the least. I often worked fourteen- and fifteen-hour days, usually seven days a week. I loved it.

I became laser-focused on succeeding. People depended on me. I did whatever it took to deliver despite the odds and obstacles. This often meant that I got home at two in the morning. I took few days off—even working public holidays—sometimes because I was called into work and other times when I was eager to visit some new philanthropic initiative. Driven by the impact I knew I was making, I soldiered on.

Once, I had a severe eye infection, which required an eye patch. One Saturday morning, I called my assistant Sita, who had become a good friend, to say she'd have to cope without me. She said that was fine and that she hoped I'd get some rest and feel better soon.

Thirty minutes later, however, she called.

"You'll have to come in, Jill," she said. "He's going crazy and throwing tantrums, and if it carries on, I'm going to have to run away!"

"But I can't, I'm in such a bad way," I replied. She pleaded and I gave in.

When I got to the office, he asked me why I hadn't come to work.

"But you can see!" I told him, pointing to the patch on my eye. "I've got a very bad infection and it's painful."

"Well, you can see out of the other eye! You don't need to work. Just be here in case I need you. Just be here and I'll forgive you."

He claimed his extremes were due to Bank of America's culture, but I knew it was him. In his world, we didn't celebrate American holidays because we were a bank based in India and didn't celebrate Indian holidays because we were an American bank.

One night, I got home at midnight, and after kicking off my shoes, despite my exhaustion, I stayed up to chat by phone with Susan since we hadn't had private time in ages. About 1:30 a.m., the doorbell rang. I answered to find my boss's driver on the other side of the door—I was needed at the bank. Off I went. The man was an incurable workaholic and turned me into one as well.

I was committed to doing this job as long as possible, determined to help those who were suffering the most. I and many others worked after hours and on weekends to transport rations to the slums in a lorry. Desperate people often mobbed us and we barely escaped with our lives. This was during the time when the plague was running rampant through the slums. It was a terrible community fate and the last thing I thought I could handle.

When I was with the poor and the needy, people on their deathbeds, and people who had no one to care for or love them, I was at my best. It was in those settings when I felt happiest and most fulfilled. I often worked until near collapse, but I couldn't bear

to see little children suffer in poverty as we had, going without food or water, being sick, or dying alone on the streets or in makeshift shelters. Making a difference in people's lives, in whatever small ways, energized me. I had never forgotten how much the small gestures of kindness in my childhood meant to me and what a difference they had made for my family. I wanted to replicate that feeling in others. This was my time to give back and I wanted to do everything in my power to help as many people as possible. The physical toll it took on me was nothing compared to the fulfillment of my life's purpose.

Jillian at Bank of America

My career and my work with the poor had begun to eclipse everything else. Any semblance of a social life was moving to the back burner. I became convinced that I didn't have space in my life for any personal relationships.

The more poverty and devastation I saw in the streets, the more my personal world recalibrated each day, and how I saw myself changed

as well. Day by day, what was becoming most important to me, what began to define me and my moral code, was steadily transforming. Looking back, it was happening in small, sometimes indiscernible increments. I was still working a traditional job. I had professional responsibilities, and I never shirked them. While I enjoyed the work, the world outside the corporate office continued to beg my attention. Often, I felt tied to a rope that kept yanking on my soul. I was edging away from one world into an entirely different one.

I often fought off distracting, intrusive thoughts during the workday. Sometimes it was the image of an animal being kicked, beaten, or having firecrackers tied to their tail; puppies being used as footballs, cats being run over, and other cruelties that were beyond human endurance. I was consumed by the singular desire to make a difference, to stop the brutality and barbarism. Maybe it was recalling an old woman, in threadbare clothes, huddling under stairs, alone, with no one to love her, her eyes sad—were they sad out of emotion or hunger? These images burned into my memory were powerful and self-sustaining. I carried them with me constantly. They didn't torment me more than they were flashes to make sure I never lost sight of a world more commanding and real than the one I inhabited during business hours. They had become the keepers of my conscience.

Seeing children in squalor, begging for something to eat to survive another day, with no place to call home other than the streets, broke my heart. The same for so many elders whose families had simply abandoned them, leaving them to die in disgrace, humiliation, and neglect. I often cried once I got home. The rampant devastation enflamed my spirit and rocked my soul. Walking through the streets, I'd look around in bewilderment, not understanding how everyone could go about their business as usual with so much suffering enveloping them and screaming for attention. It wasn't as if the poverty, sickness, disability, and approaching death were random—they were everywhere!

How does one become numb to it? What is the internal mechanism that allows a person to shut what their eyes see, snuff out what their nose smells, and ignore what their soul reflects? How could people walk past the poor and destitute and not so much as bat an eyelid?

But I knew I couldn't waste emotional energy worrying about others who did not care or share my perspective. As frustrated and often demoralized as I was about the state of the world, I knew I shouldn't judge. I wasn't naïve. Everyone has crosses to bear, my father would say. Everyone has to make choices from circumstances that are uniquely theirs. I had to worry about myself: who I was, who I should be, and, above all, what I could do. The question I began to ask myself was, could I really make a difference? Could I find my voice? And if I found it, what could I do to make it heard? For sure, acts of charity, however minuscule, made me feel fulfilled for the time being. They grounded me, defined a value system for me to live by, and were reaffirming. Each act also honored my mum and her lifelong selflessness. But that was a small part of where my mind was starting to go. I wanted to find the way forward to change the world systemically, in a way that raised the collective conscience—galvanizing communities and inspiring others to pick up the mantle of giving and kindness. The effort had to be about more than individual charitable acts, although that of course was essential. The larger mission needed to infuse cultures with a value system that would become innately generational.

The resources and networks were out there. People were already making the effort, trying to help. Pockets of the community cared. Still, I often wondered about the benefit concerts that were held, the work of the Sisters of Charity, and so much more that was being done, and yet, world poverty was pervasive and no less inescapable for the good intentions and deeds that existed to eradicate it. I wondered how we could actually solve this problem, instead of just continuing to talk about it.

If I'd learned anything by that point in my life, it was that every challenge can be overcome, tragedy can be survived, and all darkness can lead to light, even if the way forward is baby steps. Looking back, I had begun to develop a commitment to a cause, not merely of discernible goals, but how I should see myself and where I stood in the world. Still, I knew that before I could begin to affect change and make a difference in the lives of others, I had to get stronger myself. I couldn't empower others until that happened. I wanted nothing more than to help those who were incapable of helping themselves, who needed a hand in finding their own strength to fight for themselves and for what they believed in. I believed that kindness could heal a whole day, a whole year, and a whole life. But first I had to find my voice and the strength to use it.

My internal mantra was couched in words I had personally heard Mother Teresa say: that we need to stop waiting for leaders. We need to put in the work ourselves—person by person, step by step—and that is exactly what I decided to do.

The extracurricular work we were doing raised the BofA India profile, putting it on the global map for corporate charitable and diversity programs. Employees felt they were giving back in tangible, meaningful ways. I emerged as the identified face and leader of the BofA charitable initiatives in India. In recognition, the bank sent me to the worldwide headquarters in San Francisco to receive several awards. Among them was the Bank of America Individual Achievement Award, selected from charity network contributors across a group of thirty different countries. I received the award in front of a completely packed hotel ballroom. When they called my name, I tripped and fell from sheer nervousness. I share this to point out that anxiety, lack of self-confidence, and fear happen to so many of us. But if we fight through these impediments, we end up as winners.

I also received the Service Excellence award, the Bank of America Star award for dedication and commitment to the organization, and

the Global Chapter of the Year award for the publicity the bank received from the extensive charity projects undertaken in India.

The bank sent me on three global trips to publicize our charitable work. It was a rare opportunity for a girl like me, and certainly a departure from the norm. It also came with consequences. When I got back, people in some quarters suggested I was receiving preferential treatment. While many were complimentary—"She is blessed and deserves everything she's worked so hard for"—I found it hard to ignore the detractors. To my disappointment, small-mindedness existed even amongst senior professionals working for a global bank, no different in kind than the narrow-mindedness we sometimes experienced in the Kidderpore slums. I held tight to my father's words: "Let not a person's opinion of you change the opinion you have of yourself."

Harder to ignore was the whisper smear campaign that, because I was an Anglo-Indian girl, I must be sleeping with my boss. When I told him what I'd heard, he laughed and then got very serious. "Look Jillian, I am in the newspapers and on TV all the time. Many people dislike the idea of an American bank presence in India and that I, as an Indian, work for an American bank, or worse still, they dislike me for some other reason. The first mistake any employee makes, I get the blame. So, they hate the bank and wait for any opportunity to hate me too. But all I do is come to the office and do my job and get on with my work because what is said is simply people's opinions. I cannot change those, so I don't let them change me. Just do your job and know that I understand your value, and that's all that matters. Discussing or even acknowledging such behavior or talk is a disgrace to all who indulge in it and that includes you and me, too."

I learned a great lesson that day, and I never brought any more gossip to his attention. From then on, I got comfortable letting my work performance speak for me. I had come to realize that—irrespective of social, economic, or cultural background—some

people will always feel compelled to spew negative commentary and unwarranted criticism, and sometimes they'll go so far as to bully and abuse others. It still took me many years and an evolved maturity to fully grasp that such behavior has little or nothing to do with its target and often springs from entrenched insecurity and longstanding conditioning, but I was no longer bothered by the negative opinions of others.

I had turned a major corner in my life. I felt grounded like never before and poised for whatever life had in store for me.

24 | Fragile Dreams

My BofA career took off and was the clear centerpiece of my life. By the time I was settled and fully immersed in my dual position within the company, I'd been with Shane for seven years. He was a genuinely sweet and caring person, but he wasn't career-focused, which had begun to cause fissures in the relationship. I was doing exceptionally well at the bank and, unfortunately, he felt inadequate in comparison.

This situation was exacerbated when people within our social circle made snide comments about how I was doing well and he wasn't. He didn't deserve that and I told him so, but it fueled tension between us. It seemed that no matter where he went, people reminded us of the delta in our relative successes. Failing to see his better qualities and lacking sensitivity, they sometimes made him the brunt of insulting jokes. This of course said more about their character than his, but it had a damaging effect on his self-esteem.

Our problems went deeper though. We never had what most would consider a normal relationship. We bounced from dealing with my mother's terminal illness and my obsessive attention to my

younger siblings to taking care of his father who became terminally ill, bringing Santosh into our lives, and then moving my ill father from Calcutta to live with us—this all began early in our relationship, and so it was all we knew together. We were a caretaker couple. It wasn't a healthy model for building a relationship.

My priorities had also changed. I had come to the point where I was sure I wanted to devote every waking moment to people in desperate need. With each passing month, I moved deeper into charitable work, becoming steely focused on those responsibilities. I stopped giving him attention. He complained that I'd lost track of the relationship we had, and he was correct. I had failed him; I had failed us. Despite how we cared for each other emotionally, we drifted apart. People come in and out of your life for a reason, and while I once cared deeply for him, my priorities had become incompatible with our partnership. It was clear that our relationship had run its course.

One of the annual events I organised for all 300 retail and corporate employees of the bank was a weekend away to a local tourist destination, as a sort of thank you for all their hard work and effort the previous year. I arranged a trip to Agra, a short way away from our branch location in Delhi. Agra is, of course, famous for the Taj Mahal, and we were lucky to reserve almost the entire Mughal Sheraton, where the Taj was visible from the balconies and viewing galleries. It was on one of those viewing galleries I first spent time with my future husband. We just seemed to get talking one evening, and before we knew it, we realised we were the only ones left there.

The sun was about to rise, and the whole night had passed without our noticing, both of us so absorbed in conversation! I had seen him around in the bank before, but we had never really talked or interacted before that trip to Agra. He was a diligent banking professional, working fourteen- to fifteen-hour days himself, and seemed extremely focused on his career, as I was. He was intelligent

and well-read, and we clearly took to each other quite quickly, having a fair amount in common.

When we started to see each other, we were both very careful to be discreet about our relationship and not let it come in the way of our professional lives at the bank. However, word eventually got around that we were seeing each other, and whilst many people were happy for us, our relationship won him no respect from some quarters, especially when his boss found out that I was an Anglo-Indian girl—not *really* Indian. If he ever asked to leave work on time or for a rare day off, his manager would always provoke him, saying that all he wanted to do was to see the "slut" and that he did not have the ambition to work hard. This wasn't true as he was, and still remains, a very career-focused person.

Over time, he learned to look through his boorish boss's racist ranting, and it didn't hurt any longer, having dismissed it as the ignorance of a so-called professional who, sadly, had no respect for women or for anyone to that matter of fact. It did make me angry; his boss didn't even know me and, quite ignorantly, he and others like him branded me unworthy, even though they didn't know how hard I had worked to get to where I was. They did not know how much I had struggled my whole life, the sadness and grief I had buried inside me, the fact that I had two little siblings at home whom I cared for, or that I worked incredibly hard for reasons beyond my own self-interest.

Before considering any of that in the slightest, people like him just shot their mouths off in order to get their own way or make their positions—or rather, their egos—felt. Because he was a department head in the bank, he *obviously* held the right to speak and judge in the way he did, even without knowledge, experience, or fact. He never paused for a minute to think that he had no idea what he was talking about, but he knew one thing extremely well—how to abuse and degrade people just because he could.

But we rose above all that, knowing how we felt about each other, and we got engaged to be married in the year 2000. He made me truly happy because he cared enough to look after me as my parents had done. His parents were professionals of note—university professors—and although they spent part of their lives abroad, they were very much Indian at heart. This meant that even in his family I was not looked upon favourably, and neither was I readily accepted.

As is a tradition in India, my fiancé's family undertook to have my birth chart done, which said, by virtue of my date of birth, I spelt death for their son. My mother-in-law to be told me that I was a *Manglik*, which apparently means a girl who one day would be the death of her husband because we were star-crossed or something like that. While my fiancé laughed and told me not to bother about this traditional mumbo-jumbo and that he did not believe it for a second, it did hurt me that educated professionals like my future in-laws did not realise that saying this to someone when they had just got engaged was incredibly hurtful.

I understood how rare it was to be in a position like mine, but I was made to feel like they were doing me a favour or taking a risk by allowing their son to marry me. Little did I know then that the idea was to make it known that nothing and nobody were above their son and that I was coming into the family with a curse. I also started to notice differences in the way his family interacted with each other compared to the culture to which I was accustomed. Even though his mother was an intellectual in her own right and a respected university professor, she nevertheless appeared to be scared or timid most of the time when her husband was around. While visiting us, she would not serve herself or allow me to serve myself until the men had been served first. I did not understand this as my father had instilled in us that ladies were always to be put first.

I struggled for a long time to try and understand this behaviour and to accept it, but I was always very sad for his mother. I recall

several times, when I was talking to her about her son's diabetes, that whenever her husband walked in and just looked at her, she either changed the topic or simply left the room.

It felt as though I was being forced to accept that was just how things were going to be if I was part of their family and I found it extremely difficult to cope under those circumstances. I was continuously upset to see another human being treated with such little respect. To my fiancé, it was more than acceptable because he had grown up with it, but to me, it was as though I was bearing witness to another person's melancholy while not being able to do anything about it. It hurt deeply and I often tried in every way I could think of to reach out and show her that she was wanted and special.

At the time we met, my fiancé had been living with diabetes for many years. Aspiring to be a normal youngster, yearning to feel part of teenage groups, and fit in with the crowd, he didn't adhere to his physician's prescribed diet or healthy living recommendations, and therefore, his condition had worsened over time. Shortly after we got engaged, he began to suffer the onset of long-term complications—it was affecting both his optical and renal function. This was a shock to both of us, and I suddenly felt a wave of uncertainty for our future.

Shortly after we got engaged, my fiancé took my father out for dinner, and my father, usually being a man of few words, had two things to say afterward. I remember him looking at me with grave concern. "Oh, he's a proper gentleman, and I like him, but there are two issues," he began in his usual caring way. "The first is that you know he's ill. I had a friend who was diabetic, and life just gets worse and worse if not kept under control. You've already had an incredibly hard life, you've already endured too much in a very short period of time, and I just hope that you don't have to take on any more; it might be the straw that breaks the camel's back.

"Second, as much as you might have told him, he does not truly understand what you've already been through, and he has no idea of what he's about to put you through either. If my wisdom serves me correctly, you shouldn't underestimate the seriousness of his condition. By marrying him, you could be in for a lifetime of something you're not prepared to deal with. My advice to you would be not to marry him because I know just how bad it can get, and I'm concerned for you. As nice as he is, as Kipling once said, 'East is East and West is West, and never the twain shall meet.' He's very different in far too many ways, and you deserve to be with someone as loving and caring as you. God knows you deserve to be happy, not living a life where your two worlds do not connect. And that's not to mention the abundance of sorrow and sadness that could come from coping with another illness of this magnitude.

"I'm going to leave you with those words," my father concluded. "And you can figure it out for yourself. You're a big girl now, but their world and our world are very different and no matter how cultured people are, or how educated people are, there will always be differences. You are very different from him in so many ways, and I can already see that. It takes a lot more to make a marriage work than a few smiles, gifts, and dinners he may have bought you. I'm asking you to think again. I want to see you happy, not leading a life of sacrifice and endurance as you have been doing for far too long."

After speaking with my father, I told my fiancé that I needed some time to think about what I wanted to do. I remember thinking constantly about the importance of getting away to England, something we had planned to do together once we were married. "It's going to mean a new job for me in the UK, and the country itself is going to be so new for me as well," I told him, "I just need some time to come to a decision." I suggested that he follow me to the UK later, but he told me, "You know I love you and would like to come with you to make sure you settle in comfortably in the new

place. We can start our life there together." I knew he really did love me and meant what he said. At that time, I just hoped—and hope being a very big thing—that things would get better. I could never abandon someone who was good to me or someone who needed me, no matter the obstacles.

Today, I realise the power behind my father's words and believe that the best school in the world is at the feet of an elder—if only we choose to listen and learn. But I didn't. I felt as though I had no control over this decision, it was simply the way forward. I had always wanted to marry a quiet, pious man—a church mouse, as my father used to tease. I wanted to dress my children in ribbon bows and sandals and take them to church every Sunday just as my mother used to do. My mind and heart agreed; I chose to marry him and embark on whatever journey the universe had in store for us.

25 | Back to our Roots

Amid the enveloping BofA charitable activity and my banking career, I had not lost sight of an important personal goal: a promise I'd made to my mother. I committed to caring for the young ones and bringing them up well. Now I was finally earning enough money to send them to a good school and provide extra funds to improve their lives. I wanted to ensure they didn't have to face the hardships Vanessa and I had endured. Their lives would be better.

Essential to the plan was bringing all my family members to the UK. A fervent dream of my parents was relocating us to the land of our family roots. It had always hovered in the background of our lives together. No surprise then that when my father moved to Delhi to live with me, he raised that possibility again, going on about how in the UK we'd be accepted and appreciated and how life would be better for us. He never stopped wanting us to be happier.

Traveling for BofA had opened my worldly eyes. I got to see the prevalence of social tolerance in developed nations. Like India, they had diverse cultures, but unlike India, for the most part, they more

readily embraced their varied mix of people. Seeing that changed my perspective. I began to ponder seriously what it might be like for the family to relocate.

Dreams of course are one thing and execution quite another, and there was one major stumbling block. We had to establish British citizenship to engineer the exodus, which meant I'd need to locate the family's ancestry papers. I had to find birth certificates of both sets of grandparents to prove our English lineage.

I happily discovered that the couple who looked after me when I moved to Delhi had dealt with the identical challenge. They had a similar ancestry—their parents and grandparents were British—and had successfully relocated to the UK themselves a few years ago. They provided me with all the information I needed to approach the Home Office and British Library, which stored birth certificates for British people born in India at the time of the Raj.

My boss pitched in, helping me dissect the ins and outs of the paperwork. He also extended a planned business trip I had to London to afford me extra time to visit the Home Office and move the ancestral search along. It was a good start.

I paid the requisite fees, which I learned gave me a one-time search. If they found nothing based on the information I supplied, I'd have to pony up a new fee to institute a new round based on new information. Each subsequent search, with new information to input, required an additional fee.

The limited information I was initially able to offer them turned up nothing. A nagging feeling of looming failure filled my gut. But I knew one thing: I wasn't giving up. This quest had risen to the top of what was important—short-term—in my life. The problem was that I had little at my disposal. The best source, in theory, was my father. He was coming on eighty, in poor health, and his memory was fading. I *had* to get him to remember details, information buried in his subconscious that might allow me to pinpoint dates or at least

narrow the range to where the British authorities would take up the challenge in earnest.

I sat with him at night and asked questions. When did my different grandparents die, and where, and from what? Did he recall funerals or weddings? Where did they take place? What time of year? Could he see the funerals or weddings in his mind's eye? Were there any name changes along the way? Any special occasions to recall? Where did my grandparents live in the early days? What about schooling? I tried to get him to tell stories of days gone by, whether from his own experiences or tales passed on to him, to exhume his memory and visualize events to create a timeline. I drilled him for weeks on end.

While we were unable to establish precise birthdays, the laborious memory exercises yielded more clues than I had before. I had narrowed the gap and so rolled the dice on a second search. With the help of a lovely and accommodating lady at the Home Office, we managed to get my parents' birth certificates from the British Library. Getting certificates for their parents, without dates of birth, was more problematic. I implored her to keep looking. She said she'd do her best.

Imagine my joy when she told me she'd found the other birth certificates. She also somehow managed to find the marriage certificates. A blocked road had been freed of all impediments. We had a complete ancestral chain proving our British lineage. I sent her a bouquet.

She mailed the certificates by courier and, when they arrived in India, the family was ecstatic. The Haslam odyssey to England had officially begun. It was like winning the lottery!

I relayed the news to my boss at BofA. He was genuinely happy. He was leaving as well. It was a new day for both of us. He focused on what was to come next.

"I'll be leaving BofA myself soon, and I want you to be able to go at the same time," he said. "You've been here for over five years

now and you've been good to us, so I'm going to see if the bank will consider awarding you a severance package. It will help you with all your expenses when you settle there. If anyone deserves to succeed, you do, and I will be there to help you every step of the way. I want the best for you."

The severance package was very generous and exceeded my expectations, sending waves of gratitude throughout my system as I recalled the dark days of living under the stairs or when we could not afford 100 rupees for Kidderpore rent or even five rupees for a meal.

By the time we were ready to leave, my father's health had taken a downturn, rendering him too ill to travel. We would have to leave him in India for the time being and await the day he'd improve enough to travel. Leaving him behind, if for a short while, made departing bittersweet. My father was unfazed; he beamed with excitement to see us leave. He saw the move to the UK as the fulfillment of a long-burning family mission. The family had overcome extraordinary hurdles and made it successfully to the other side. It was a day of great reckoning.

Still, I could tell he was hurting. Another part of him, down deep, wanted nothing more than for me to stay with him. Our freedom left him isolated. He had Santosh, who would take good care of him, but now his children were about to leave him for an uncertain future apart.

As we left, he said: "I do not know how to thank you for everything you've done for me and the family, and for so many around you. I know one day you will be blessed with more than you will ever need. Never, ever, give up your dreams. Continue to be who you are."

The transition to life in London—the move itself, acclimating to a new job, and basking in the excitement that comes with new beginnings—had, for a time, dominated my life view. It was literally a dream come true. My parents had never lost sight of the ultimate prize in the family journey: that their children might

someday migrate from India to the land of their ancestry. It burned in their hearts, fueling their lives, and propelling them forward—a bright light to follow. And now it had become a reality.

It is hard to overstate the power of fulfilling a dream of that magnitude against the backdrop of what we'd endured. It was more than simply checking a box on a wish list. It was a life-empowering achievement, testimony to how resilience holds the promise of untold gifts in the face of daunting obstacles and dimming hope.

Still, standing proudly on UK soil as a newly minted British citizen and permanent resident, I never lost sight of how the journey remained incomplete. While the fervent yearning of my parents to return arm-in-arm to visit the UK could never be realized with the passing of my mother, the opportunity lingered for my father. His personal dream was still alive. I had to get him to the UK for a visit.

The problem was his health. Now eighty, he had become frail, seemingly cheating death each day with his fragile heart. Not surprisingly, his doctors forbade him to travel, concerned that the rigors of such a trip could easily be the final straw. Their advice was to wait and allow him to gain enough strength to withstand the journey. They were hopeful it could happen. *Let time do its thing. Be patient.* I took a deep breath and waited with keen anticipation.

In the meantime, I continued my search for any surviving members of his family to make his triumphant return that much sweeter. I had tried to locate them when I was gathering ancestral materials to obtain our British citizenship but time and again ran into dead ends. I came away convinced that all aunts and uncles on both sides of the family had died, leaving my father the last standing family head in the ancestral lines.

Then, the door opened a sliver, bringing in a ray of light. My father found an old letter from his sister Dorothy Finnerty, whom he called Dolly. The only contact information the letter contained was

an address from the distant past, but it was new information and, while a thin reed, something to go on. The letter breathed new life into our dormant quest.

Lo and behold, I eventually discovered that Auntie Dolly was still alive, spending her final chapter in an assisted living facility in London. I was thrilled. Wasting no time, I went to visit her unannounced, taking Susan with me. I could hardly restrain the combination of emotions. I was about to visit an aunt whom I had never met and who may not know I existed. My mind caromed between thoughts and my heart between emotions, as I struggled to get a handle on what to expect. I knew, implicitly, that the experience could land anywhere on a spectrum from heartbreak to boundless joy.

My husband was kind enough to drive us there, and upon arrival at the facility, I learned that my aunt was ninety years old and in poor health. I became increasingly anxious waiting in the anteroom while the staff alerted her (and her visiting daughter, my cousin) that she had a surprise guest, and not any guest, but the daughter of her younger brother Roland. The poor thing must have been absolutely stunned at first and then, I imagined, channeled a tsunami of emotion on the news. She, too, could have no way of knowing what to expect.

As I was ushered into her room, I found her sitting with her daughter, looking comfortable on a couch covered with throw pillows. She was bright-eyed and looking eager. I stopped midway into the room to take in the surroundings. It was a well-appointed room, complete with plants, flowers, wall hangings, and an array of colors. I could sense nervousness flooding my face. It must have been apparent, for my aunt smiled broadly, setting me more at ease, and in her eyes and soft smile, I saw my father. The resemblance was unmistakable, and I absorbed it into my heart. She stretched her arms out to me. I went over, sat next to her so she didn't have to stand, and gave her a warm and strong hug. It was so strong, I could feel her recoil

uneasily, more out of surprise from the passion of my embrace. She was, after all, British raised, and as that culture went, more reserved. We Indians tend to display our emotions prominently on our sleeves and are decidedly more "touchy-feely." Susan and I couldn't hide our enthusiasm. We were both overwhelmed. Indeed, inside I was giddy. Auntie was much more grounded. She tempered the moment.

Jillian' and Susan with their dad's sister Dolly in London

Still, I could tell that in her own way she was over the moon with excitement. Her eyes said it all—eyes I'd seen often before. What struck me too was how much she had her wits about her. She was sharp, responsive, understood who we were, and never failed to address us by name.

I engaged her in conversation, at first haltingly, and eventually to where we found a rhythm together. As we did, we each filled in the deep historical gaps from our respective lives. I was mindful to underscore the positive in our family background and downplay the negative. Even though she asked about my father—she was understandably thrilled to learn he was alive—I didn't disclose the state of his health or his tortured history of cardiac problems. Nor did I mention the lost family children. It was an occasion for joy that I didn't want to puncture with tales of woe.

When I told her my father was planning to visit the UK, she let her guard down for the first time, succumbing to soft happy tears that filled her eyes. She had naturally assumed he had long passed—as had everyone else on her side of the family—and hearing she'd get to see her long-lost younger brother was a lot to process. She struggled to contain herself, doing her best to keep that reserved countenance. I couldn't imagine what she was feeling. But I knew this much: it was a glorious moment.

We stayed for about two hours. At the end, I promised my aunt I'd bring my father to her and let her know once I had finalized travel plans. We hugged again—more softly this time, but no less warmly—and Susan and I were off.

When we left the facility, I don't think my feet touched the ground. I was flying. To connect with a member of our family, an experience I'd never imagined was even a remote possibility, was a blessing and an extraordinary gift.

My father was quite pleased to hear about the visit, although, characteristically, like his sister, he didn't flood me with overt emotions. I could tell from his voice how happy he was and how much he looked forward to reuniting with his older sister. We had come a long way.

Meanwhile, my father's health began to improve to where a trip to London had become more than possible; it was probable.

Plans got underway. The idea was for him to stay with my husband, Neil, Susan, and me. We had the space. I was eager to make the arrangements.

Things got complicated when my in-laws told us they wanted to make their first London visit. Fair enough I thought. They could come visit and stay with us once my father settled in. I was sure my father wouldn't mind. It would be an opportunity for them to meet and get better acquainted. But when they heard my father was coming ahead of them, and would be visiting with us when they arrived, they insisted on visiting before he came. They reasoned that my husband, as the man in the family, had the right to have his parents come before my father.

At first, I was beside myself with frustration. It was difficult for me to get my head around how they saw the world and I struggled with their value system. More than that, I couldn't understand their lack of empathy. They knew my father was ill. They also knew I had recently contacted his sister after more than a sixty-year family hiatus. They knew, or should have realized, how much his coming to the UK meant to me.

I was hoping my husband would step in and set things right. But he was still laboring under the weight of his medical struggles, and he didn't want to complicate things with his parents. He preferred the path of least resistance. He felt that it was easier to let them visit and then bring my father over after. We had waited this long to bring him. A relatively short delay was no big deal.

I capitulated, and we put off my father's visit to allow his parents to come first. They visited, stayed a few weeks, and left. Once they were gone, I returned my attention to making travel arrangements for my father.

The planning was short-lived. As I put the pieces together for my father's relocation, I received word from Santosh in Delhi that my father had passed away. Santosh was still living with him and

caring for him at the time. He told me that after hearing a loud, disconcerting gasp, he rushed upstairs to my father's bedroom to discover that my father had passed away. It was March 27, 2002.

I was profoundly sad. Death is always hard to handle, but this had a different feel now that both my parents had passed. The two-family rocks were gone from us, along with their deep wells of wisdom. We were on our own more than ever. I was comforted knowing my father had lived the best life he could, dedicating himself to his family. Like my mother, he stood for something, and together they had embraced and honored bedrock human values of compassion and generosity.

Not surprisingly, as the funeral approached and I began to deal with the early pangs of missing him, I felt regret swelling from deep within for not standing up to my in-laws and insisting that my father visit when he was ready to come. I should have put a firm foot down. I arranged to go to Delhi for the funeral and, once there, buried my father with love, pride, and gratitude—and deep sadness. I felt I had failed him.

I knew that upon my return to London I should circle back and report to my aunt. But that was easier said than done. Timidity quickly set in. I feared that delivering news of my father's death would almost certainly break my aunt's heart and crush her spirits with huge disappointment. I struggled to summon the courage to overcome the fear that was beginning to consume me. Weighing equally heavily on me was shame—I hadn't fulfilled my promise to reunite her with her long-lost younger brother. I became frozen, procrastinated, and never acted.

Regret can be a powerful inhibitor. I took some comfort knowing I'd injected small doses of happiness and hope into the lives of my aunt and father. I'd also made a connection that I'm sure no one in the family ever imagined possible. Both were positive marks I could exalt to sap any inclination I felt to become mired in

remorse. It was a perspective that allowed me to focus on the lessons I could learn from the situation and reflect on how important it is to stand up for myself no matter what others say or think. I had to stay centered on being my own person, directing my own life, and fulfilling my life's mission.

26 | Heeding the Call

When I left India, I was in a great place professionally. I was running the country manager's office for BofA and was designated as the head of the employee charity and diversity network. I was also appointed as a public relations officer and had my own assistant. Senior management valued and appreciated me and compensated me generously, equal to other bank executives. When I arrived in the UK, I was eager to resume my banking career and expand my professional horizons, but I was told that, because I had no London experience, I would have to start again at the bottom. So I joined ABN Amro, a Dutch bank that later became The Royal Bank of Scotland (RBS), as a personal assistant—a position I thought I was done with years ago. This was a huge blow to my confidence, but I knew that relenting to feelings of hopelessness would do nothing to bring me closer to achieving my goals.

As I had done at Bank of America, I went straight for the online training resources and would sit for hours after work and go in early to make my way through those courses. Firstly, they were free and offered to all employees of the bank, and secondly,

it was knowledge, education, and world-class content provided by a prestigious global bank. I felt incredibly fortunate and took advantage of the resources at my disposal. It was a tremendous opportunity to learn about advanced presentation skills, effective communication, leadership skills, strategic thinking, elements of good judgment, the disciplines of high performing and super-productive people, and hundreds more eye-opening subjects. There were times when I couldn't wait to leave for work at 7 a.m. and get to the bank to start my training. Determined to get ahead, I became obsessed with learning more about the fascinating world of success and advancement. As I gained new skills and knowledge, I steadily progressed to running the administrative operations and support functions across three floors of the global corporate office in London. I had stayed the course, taken my lumps, and climbed my way back up that ladder.

Yet, something was missing, and I knew it had nothing to do with career satisfaction. Matthew 22:14 kept coming back to me: "For many are called, but few are chosen." I tried hard to make sense of it all and the best way that I can explain it is this: there is always a call that needs to be answered, but not many will rise to answer it. I was clearly not doing what my heart called on me to do: to make a difference in the lives I cared most about. I had put all of that on hold to execute our relocation to the UK and get my career back on track, but now the time had come to resume the pursuit of my life's mission.

The first step I took was to volunteer during my lunch hour, teaching kids in the poorer and most deprived areas of London, and eventually, I was able to assist their families on weekends as well. I began to make contacts and build relationships. The more immersed I became in these communities, the more I called up the world my siblings and I had inhabited for so long. I felt a powerful kindred bond with the children I was helping.

When I first visited the UK, I was captivated by the country I'd only heard and read about and marveled at the toy-like homes and the cleanliness of it all. But whenever I found myself admiring the green fields, endless forests, expansive palaces, and gorgeous landscapes I saw in the UK, I couldn't help thinking of the millions who lived cheek-by-jowl in the slums or families who lived with eight to twelve members packed together in one room. Having seen these severe contrasts with my own eyes, I became fixated on the unfairness of the world. I wondered how rich and powerful countries and their leaders could allow such inequality and suffering—especially in their own backyards. We display examples of this suffering on television, social media, and elsewhere for all the world to see, and still millions of people go without shelter, food, or any hope at all.

I was once sitting in a business class lounge when a woman came in with the trolly and bin and started emptying all of the food from the giant buffet into the bin. I walked up to her and asked what was wrong with the food. It looked perfectly fine, so why was she throwing it all away? She said that her instructions were that, after a certain amount of time had passed, it was her duty to replenish the buffet. I couldn't contain my anguish and burst out crying. She stopped and asked, "Have I upset you?" I just said to her, "The only words that come to me right now are, 'Father forgive them for they know not what they do.'" She put her hand on my arm and said, "I am a Christian too, and it pains me to do this job, but it is beyond my control." I pressed her hand and barely managed to say, "I understand." I went back to my seat and couldn't stop crying. The amount of food being thrown away in that one lounge each day could feed several families in the slums for weeks. Thinking of how much joy that food would bring to children living on the brink of starvation broke my heart.

At home in the UK, we do much of our grocery shopping online. On several occasions, someone else's groceries have been delivered to us by accident. The first time it happened, we called the supermarket right away to have them come retrieve the mixed-up groceries and what we were told was almost impossible to comprehend. They told us to just throw the entire order away because they weren't allowed to take it back once it had been delivered, but not to worry—they would send someone with our order as soon as they could. We've tried to catch the delivery person before they drive away, but even then, it is considered too late.

My sister works in a school and is often reduced to tears by what she witnesses in the lunchroom. All of the food that does not get eaten is thrown away after the children leave the room. Some of them do eat the food, but many of them take it and just throw it away because they prefer burgers or pizzas. Enough to feed hundreds is thrown away each day—just in that one school— without a second thought for the millions of children dying of starvation on this very planet.

It is likely difficult for most people to understand what it feels like to eat something as seemingly insignificant as a biscuit when you've been battling starvation, pushed to the brink of despair and suicide. I have been on the receiving end of such treasures, like when a local vendor would give us a sweet or roti when we had eaten not so much as a crumb for days. In those moments, a biscuit is more than a biscuit—it is hope itself.

During one of my visits to the slums in India, I met a little girl who'd been sexually molested and was covered with ringworm. I took her to the hospital and stayed with her while she got medical attention. When I asked her if she could hold my hand and try to walk, her mother told me that she hadn't eaten for two days and was too weak. I was furious. I wanted to take her home and feed her and keep her hidden, afraid she might be abused again or left hungry if

she returned to the slum. Overcome with feelings of futility, I felt that my attempts to help were but drops in the ocean.

The reality of what is out there, even a fraction of the suffering I have witnessed, would shock the world if only it cared enough to open its collective eyes. I have seen little ones as young as two and three years old trying to awaken their parents who have passed away from sheer exhaustion. Hordes of people weak from starvation, unable to open their mouths to eat; and those who—and this is so painful to write—severed their limbs in exchange for a meal, intentionally blinded their children so others would take pity on them and give them more money, or sold their organs in order to survive another day. For many families, enduring such devastation is the only way of life they've ever known, and without the means to stay together, they are torn apart physically, emotionally, and spiritually. My family was almost there too and I understand what forces parents to even contemplate paying such a price.

To my profound disappointment, I have also found that some people running charities deceive the poor. I witnessed this firsthand when I headed the charity network at Bank of America. It is not uncommon for those in control to become financially self-interested and use the organization as a tool for their self-aggrandizement. Some founders lose sight of the charitable mission they originally set out to accomplish when their organization starts bringing in substantial contributions from donors. School administrators have openly admitted to me that they cannot educate poor children together with rich children because the rich would stop sending their children to their school, which would financially damage their operations. When that mentality prevails, the *business* of charities overshadows their sacred work.

Many charities are well-intentioned and dedicated. No question. But they are nowhere near enough to help even one-tenth of those in need.

I did what I could within the parameters of BofA's charitable networks, then later through RBS, but time and time again I kept coming back to the sobering reality that my efforts were insufficient and I had to do more if I really wanted to improve the lives of those in serious need the world over. I wanted to move my support and involvement to a much greater level but I still had my own personal issues to confront. If I was truly to be of service to others, I would first need to put on my own oxygen mask.

27 | Finding My Voice

The memory of my mum, of her resilience and selflessness, remained intertwined with my spirit. Wherever she was, I wanted to show her, in my own way, that her life was not in vain. Despite her hardships, she always sought to help as many people as possible. I intended to build on her legacy.

My long-term plan was to start a business that helped people find effective paths toward better, more successful lives. Years of banking experience and training skills would come in handy, but there was so much more for me to learn about leading others to success. And though I was no longer as timid as I once was, I still had to learn not just how to be heard but to be understood. So, I enrolled in various professional training courses, including neuro-linguistic programming (NLP), a coaching/mentoring certification, public speaking, and a leadership excellence program.

The first challenge was that these trainings took place in Scotland. I would need to take the train after work every Friday, from London to Edinburgh, and spend the entire weekend in training. When I sat down on that train for the first time, I wondered if I had gone mad. My

mind raced with endless questions: Had childhood undernourishment impaired the development of my brain, and if so, was there a way to compensate for that? Were there unanticipated obstacles ahead that could end it all for me as they had for my mother? Could I realistically sustain this new lifestyle long enough to achieve my goals?

I spent the rest of the five-hour trip contemplating all of the things I had endured to be sitting on that train. I called up the memory of how I'd mixed Susan's medicine with watered-down milk from the tea shop to save her life. My parents and their unwavering determination to create something better for their children from the terrible hand they'd been dealt. Vanessa on the other side of my roach-infested torture chamber, coaching me to stay calm. The family's journey to the UK. All of the things we had accomplished against the worst odds had led me to that very moment. Wasn't I living proof that with the proper mindset, any challenge could be overcome? I was determined to find out.

When I was young, my dad always said, "No matter your start, your end is up to you. You must learn when to bend a little and when to never give up." This was an invaluable lesson about making important decisions—decisions that could change everything in an instant. More than anything I wanted to change the world, to make it a better place for the people I loved so much, and this decision was the important next step toward making that dream a reality.

So, for nearly two years, sometimes through knee-deep snow, bone-rattling cold winds, and heavy rains—weather conditions a world apart from the oppressive heat in India—I left work on Friday and traveled to Scotland in pursuit of my dreams. Each time I flirted with giving up, I drew upon the words of William Barclay who said, "Endurance is not just the ability to bear a hard thing but to be able to turn it into glory." I wrote the two lines on a notecard I kept in my purse. They infused me with confidence and the drive to take each important next step.

I stayed up nearly every night studying, getting by on even less sleep than I had in the past. I made flashcards on my lunch breaks and prepared my lessons on the train. I read as many books as I could and attended every training event my schedule allowed. It was grueling and exhausting—and transformational. I became a learning sponge. With every new skill I absorbed, my confidence and sense of purpose expanded.

The day I delivered my first paid speech to students at a nearby high school, my sister Susan was pacing the room waiting for me to return to tell her all about my experience. When I got back home, I could not hide my delight. I was finally conquering my fears and realizing my potential. After having delivered so many free speeches and trainings just to get up the ladder, it felt amazing to finally get paid, but it also meant that people believed in me and felt my speaking skills were worth paying for. I was paid sixty pounds and Susan was so proud of me, given all that I had been through and all the hard work that I had put in, that she took the sixty pounds and left the house and returned with it framed. It was the most precious things that anyone had done for me and I still have that sixty pounds in a frame with me to this day.

The £60 earned from my first paid speech framed by Susan

My professional training deepened my insight into the human condition and the functioning of the human mind far better than I could ever have imagined. I consumed book after book on the human brain

and set about learning all that I possibly could in the area of self-development, survival, adversity, resilience, and success.

Understanding the internal functioning of the human brain from a scientific perspective was all well and good, but I also wanted to know the internal personal dynamics that control whether we stay ordinary or transform to the extraordinary. If we *each* have attributes to succeed—as I was taught—why doesn't everyone give full expression to their dreams? I wanted to know if I could work on a certain part of the brain to push the boundaries of success. Could I learn what it takes to get to the top? Could I take brain medicine? I was willing to do whatever it took!

After years of study and hard work, I became qualified as a coach with a distinction, a corporate and NLP master trainer, and an author. I cut back my hours at the bank to work on starting my own training business where I helped businesses and other organizations train their employees to become leaders and innovators. It was an exhilarating journey. I finally had the necessary qualifications to help others overcome adversity and find their own path to success. I also recognized how my own life experiences could help motivate others. Authentic, personal storytelling works like magic when it comes to helping other people make changes in their own lives.

As a professional trainer, I learned how to structure and deliver talks and presentations in a way that would allow people to reflect on their own lives and then take decisive action. If I could go from living under a flight of stairs with no hope in sight to becoming a banker, an entrepreneur, a trainer, an author, and a philanthropist, I honestly believed that anyone could.

Speaking to people in a closed room with a structured presentation made me anxious enough but to be able to tailor my message to suit different audiences in universities, corporations, or conferences was a whole different ball game. However, a professional speaking platform seemed an effective way to continue my work on a larger scale. If I

was able to generate revenue from public speaking, I could help even more people, and bigger events with larger audiences would allow me to impact the world at large. The old me would have turned away from such a challenge, but the new me envisioned the rewards and decided it was worth a shot, despite my jitters.

Once again, there were serious questions I needed to ask myself. Where did my fear stem from? What is it that weakens me and what is it that strengthens me and what is it that could help me push past those obstacles?

I researched an organization called Toastmasters whose tag line read, "Where Leaders are Made." Working in the banking industry had given me many skills to help elevate my career, but this was the exact next component I needed. This was a place where I could develop advanced communication and leadership skills. The training program would take ten years, after which I would be a Distinguished Toastmaster with certification as a world-class communicator, leader, and speaker. I seized the opportunity, ignoring the voice in my head that said it would be too difficult. That voice was starting to hold less power over me, I was starting to notice, and there was a new, stronger voice that was taking over, which told me I really could accomplish anything.

All of my experience up to that point gave me valuable perspective: I understood the value of a good education in the broadest sense, the value of a good mentor, and the value of asking for help. I joined the Global Speakers Federation (GSA), the National Speaking Association (NSA), and the Professional Speaking Association (PSA) so I could learn from some of the best leaders and speakers on the planet.

It was at a PSA event in London where I met a senior member and Toastmaster named Bob Ferguson. We developed a good rapport and I asked him to mentor me. He agreed on one condition: I had to sign up for a speaking contest that was being held in six weeks.

The platform was designed to provide a speaking experience to new members and a way to receive feedback from PSA members in an open room forum. I would be competing with other professional speakers. My gut urged me to say no. *Maybe I should just give up the mentoring/speaking thing for now.* But the event was six weeks away and Bob prevailed on me to enter my name to keep the option open.

For weeks, I slept fitfully. I was so nervous. I'd awake in a cold sweat, struggling to come to terms with standing on a stage in front of an auditorium-sized audience and leaving myself open to their opinions and feedback. Many people fear public speaking more than death and faced with this new, scarier challenge, I was once again jostling for the head of that line. But I knew that if I wanted to motivate others to follow in my footsteps—to find their voices and to overcome their fears—I simply had to lead by example. As Gandhi had instructed, I would be the light that I wished to see in others.

Step by step, with Bob's skillful assistance, I developed my first public speech for the contest, which I titled, "A Winning Hand." It told the tale of Susan's birth and survival. Bob helped me stay focused and steady. Amazingly, the chairman of the PSA remarked, "Jillian, I am honoured to give your speech 10 out of 10."

Speaking opportunities started coming my way. I was invited to speak at some of the most prestigious venues and elite educational institutions like Cambridge, Kings College London, Heriot-Watt University, Durham University, and many others. In the corporate world, I spoke at the Bank of England, McDonald's, Nova Nordisk, PwC, and several others. I chaired and served as chief guest at major events, delivered six TEDx speeches, and attended venues I wouldn't have dreamt of while growing up in India.

To be sure, speaking to audiences full of bright minds and successful people didn't come easy to me. With Bob's patient mentoring, I overcame my nerves by repeatedly telling myself like a mantra that I could make it happen if I accepted the challenge.

I delivered my first ever TEDx speech in Ireland entitled, "Never Give Up and Other Complete Rubbish," and was surprised when it received over 50,000 views in a matter of hours. I knew then I was onto something. This also gave me the determination to work even harder along my ten-year journey to becoming a professional speaker.

Over time, I had emerged with a series of steps, various leaps of faith, and small measurable accomplishments. Starting my own business was an accomplishment to be sure, but getting on the speaking circuit—standing in front of hundreds of strangers—turned the corner for me, opening doors I never thought possible. I now had undeniable proof that self-belief, hard work, and tenacity could align purpose, passion, and action and give expression to any dream.

I was on the right path and making great strides. But I had not yet arrived where I belonged. The best was yet to come.

28 | Taking Others with Me

The exposure from being on the public speaking circuit, the success of my training business, and the release of my first book led to personal recognition, and while I naturally felt affirmed by the largely positive public reception, at bottom I recoiled from the attention. I felt it detracted from the many others who had helped and it also diverted attention from the vast community we were serving. One print media piece even called me the "real Slumdog Millionaire," which put the focus on how much I earned rather than the work we were doing. Instead of getting called to speak about the power of resilience, I became inundated with requests for money, letters from people who were ill, dying, suffering, and threats if I failed to help them. My intention in sharing my experience had been to show others what was possible with the right mindset and dedication. I did receive a few bookings but it was nothing compared to the barrage of abuse, threats and much more from people who hadn't even read my book and had no idea what I had been through.

I left India because my father insisted that a better life awaited us beyond its borders. But even though I had physically relocated, my

heart and soul never left the country and the people I owed so much to. People often comment about how much time I spend in Calcutta. The reality is, there will never be a time when help isn't needed. And the blight of poverty, disease, chronic illness, and lack of opportunity affecting people in countries all over the world can't be effectively addressed if the developed world does not agree to reach back and help others along the way.

With so many people in dire need of support, I knew I had to find more ways to help. I wanted to emphasize educational support, to build new foundations for men, women, and children. I aimed to help the poor from every generation. So, I set up six programs through my family's Remedia Trust: Empowering Girls, which provides girls with vocational training and the skills to start their own businesses; E3: Education, Employability, and Empowerment helps equip young people in India with job skills and life skills; Aging Smiles is dedicated to bringing food, medicine, love, and support to India's elderly homeless population who've been abandoned and forgotten; India's Disabled is designed to help a shunned segment of the Indian population with the basic needs of food, water, and hygiene; Happy Hearts provides the precious children in the slums with an education and the kind of help and support that many children receive at private schools; and the Mother Teresa Project aims to carry out the great saint's mission to care for and uplift the poorest of the poor by providing food, teaching employable skills, individual coaching, counseling, and restoring hope—one person at a time.

Soon awards started coming my way. In 2012, I received the first runner-up award for The Asian Woman of the Year in the Social and Humanitarian category. In early 2015, The Telegraph of Calcutta presented me with The True Legend award for exceptional contribution to social and humanitarian causes. In mid-2015, I was recognized as a finalist for the Role Model of the Year award for

delivering talks to educational institutes across the UK. And in late 2016, I received an award for Excellence in Humanitarianism.

Then, in 2017, I received a letter saying that I had won the Mother Teresa Memorial International Award. I was so awed by this I had to sit down and reread the letter several times. I wasn't even sure I was eligible for such an award since I wasn't Catholic. I told my family I didn't want to attend the ceremony to accept the award. I felt undeserving. My family was so proud and urged me to go, reasoning that the award would further fuel my charitable mission and shine a bright light on Remedia Trust. After much coaxing and handwringing, I agreed to go.

I arrived underdressed, to say the least. It was quite the gala affair with processions along the street led by the police and attended by government ministers—far too much publicity for me. As I approached the entrance, my mind was running a ticker tape of what all that money could do if it were put toward direct charitable efforts. I couldn't help imagining what Mother Teresa would say about such a lavish event. "Stop giving out awards in my name. Get to work and help the people in desperate need!"

Then I pictured her leading the event's presenters, officials, and attendees through the streets—just a short walking distance from the award venue—to witness with their own eyes the children, elders, disabled, and chronically ill enduring incessant hunger and unsanitary conditions; sleeping outside on dusty, smelly, noisy streets, near public drains exposed to the rapacious behavior of thieves, murderers, and gangs, struggling each day just to survive. Once again, I found myself struck by the severe juxtaposition of the haves and the have nots.

Of course, there is value in honoring people who make important charitable contributions and recognizing their selflessness. But surely, I thought, there had to be other ways to honor them while making better use of the money.

Receiving the Mother Teresa Memorial International Award

I was eventually able to enjoy the event, despite my initial misgivings. Seven high priests from seven different faiths at the Saint Teresa Church in Calcutta presented me with the award, as well as a frame of her image blessed at her tomb. After the award ceremony, the police led us through the streets of the city as part of a memorial peace rally to commemorate the twentieth anniversary of Mother Teresa's death. As I walked, I was surrounded by women and girls from the community. We smiled and chatted with each other along the route to Mother House. Looking at these bright young girls with their whole lives ahead of them, I thought about how my tiny, hungry self would have been dazzled by all of it. Little Jillu would not have believed that she would be attending such an event, and as an honoree no less.

I felt my mother was with me as I walked through the streets of the city where we had fought to stay alive and stay together for so many years. She was truly everywhere I looked, and I hoped that, wherever she was, she could see that all I had accomplished, every

project I undertook to help others, was because of the bright light of her spirit leading my way.

Surrounded by the peaceful, loving, good-hearted people in our procession, and the many others waving from the sides of the road, I called up one of my father's most uttered phrases, "We all have our crosses to bear, but that doesn't mean we must bear them alone!" I smiled and in my mind's eye I could see him beaming at me, his arm waving emphatically with joy just like he had when he watched us leave for the UK.

It was a great honour to be given the opportunity to place a wreath on Mother Teresa's grave

When we arrived at Mother House, the award committee bestowed on me another great honor; they invited me to place a wreath and an Indian flag on her tomb. I was deeply moved. Then I was invited to step into Mother Teresa's lodging—a simple tiny room with a single bed. They allowed me to spend a few moments inside by myself. I remember holding my breath as I stepped over the threshold.

Entering the small sacred space, I felt a well of emotions rising inside my chest. I wondered if maybe she had come back here to rest and pray after presenting Vanessa and me with a bag of powdered milk and bread all those years ago. Looking around, I knew I would forever hold this as one of the most precious moments of my life and though the room contained very few adornments, I found it to be a truly beautiful place. After one last look, I collected myself with a deep breath and rejoined the celebration filled to the brim with gratitude.

Epilogue

In reading this book about one family's humble struggles, you have become a witness to a story—among millions just like it—that some believed was a story not worth knowing. Hatred and ignorance tell their victims that they are not worthy of being seen, let alone worthy of love and understanding. This is the juxtaposition of values inherent in class warfare and the evils of discrimination and abuse.

The journey we've just taken together may well have prompted you to think about the conditions under which you grew up and compare them with mine. I hope, most sincerely, that yours were *entirely* different.

My path to adulthood was not an easy one, but I do not seek sympathy. Telling my story doesn't make me sad for myself because I know that my childhood is not unique; not then and not now.

This book is about prejudice and the sadness and suffering it causes. But it is, above all, about resilience and finding the mental strength to get back up every time the rug of life is pulled from under your feet. It was not an easy book to write, and retelling some of the more disturbing stories of my childhood was like tearing open old

scar tissue, but I hope you found that amongst all the sadness there is goodness, hope, and love and that the part you carry with you is the determination to improve and succeed, driven by the capacity to overcome and to heal and, most of all, to forgive.

Light *can* come from darkness. My family's pain is not the entire tale, nor is it the end of the story. My desire for you is that you have learned things you can use to make your own life better and recognise that it is ultimately hope that is powerful enough to permeate even the darkest of places.

My story is not a cautionary tale from a long, lost world; it reflects the realities of humanity *today*, and I hope when you close this book you feel wiser, and perhaps a little more compassionate towards those who are much less fortunate than you—for even being able to read a book is a privilege many will never know. Against some of the worst odds, I have changed my life—found my voice to be heard for the betterment of others—and want to help as many as I possibly can to do the same.

We now have a bond, you and I, a bond built from acknowledging some truths of history that are rarely told. My heartfelt wish is that my cross to bear aids those who need inspiration and soothes those disturbed by intolerance. If through this book—and my work today which grew out of this story—I can make a difference in other people's lives, then I will die a happy person. I really do not require anything more.

With love and thanks,

Jillian

Afterword

I regularly return to India to visit the place where I grew up in Calcutta. A basic truth draws me there. Inside the most devastating of living conditions exists pervasive kernels of kindness that separate the poorest from many segments of our world. Being there reminds me that the most profound virtue in life is the smallest tendering of a good deed.

In the days of my youth, kindness was embodied in vendors who offered us a sweet, meat bones for broth, a tiny loaf of stale bread, or overripe tomatoes they couldn't sell.

That kindness was inside the man who gave us ash to wash our dishes, the owner of the tea shop who filled our tiny bowl with diluted milk to save Susan's life, the tailor who gave us scraps of cloth, and the local chemist who gave us free medicines when we were in dire need. It was found in the sponsors who allowed my sisters and me to attend school tuition-free and in the gestures of friends and neighbors who gave us a rupee or two here and there to buy something to eat, a torn blanket they no longer needed, an old pencil, a decent pair of knickers, and sometimes a place to sleep. It even found expression in

Mrs. Evans who gave us stairs to live under, Mrs. Brown who took us in, and dare I say, the men who made us dance for a little treat.

Each of them, in varying degrees and ways, found a place within themselves to treat us as fellow human beings, small children, parents, and a struggling family needing help to get to the next day or week. Each showered us with gestures of kindness that cleansed us and provided rays of hope that ignited our will to survive. The loving responses of that smattering of people, who may have forgotten us, I will never forget.

I cherish the invaluable words from Elton John's song, "The Circle of Life," indeed, we should never take more than we give. They call to mind the community of poor people who never have much but always share what they do have.

I am drawn to the streets of my youth also because it is where I found the internal strength to survive, how I became fortified to meet whatever impediments life chose to throw my way, the place the most important of life lessons percolated and begged attention, and where my core value system developed and solidified. It is a place—despite its rampant poverty and squalor unfit for pigs—I will forever hold sacred as my home.

My parents repeatedly extolled the value of gratitude, that we should be grateful for everything we had, for life was a blessing, no matter how sad the conditions or how prevalent the abuse and daily suffering. Returning to Calcutta each time is an illuminating passage down a corridor replete with a mix of dark, heartbreaking, and happy memories. Each experience is a wonderful reminder that we should never look down on another person, never feel ashamed of our past, and be forever vigilant in being self-honest and aware.

I have learned much about how the human mind influences our actions and I have applied what I have learned to understanding myself better. The introspection enhances my ability to help others. I know we can improve lives, regardless of how futile prospects sometimes

seem. We need only the right learning methods, commitment, guidance, and support. Remedia today has helped educate hundreds of children, spawned over two hundred projects, served over five thousand clients, and won thirteen awards. We are impervious to the color of one's skin and beholden to the splendor of the soul.

I wrote this book less to share my story than to inspire others to realize their unfavorable circumstances don't need to be their reality. Hardships can be overcome and turned into unimaginable success. In the words of Mark Caine: "The first step towards success is taken when you refuse to be a captive of the environment in which you first find yourself." I hope that, in reading this book, you will become more aware, more resilient, and willing to give *your life* your all. No matter our background, we each have a distinctive story to tell.

I continue to try to repay the kindness shown to me and to live up to the standards my parents established for their children through my philanthropic work. Helping others heals our own pain and can be a powerful coping mechanism. I want to help others find their voice as I found mine. That is my life mission.

May we all find the courage to step outside of what holds us back and give full life to the purpose we are here to realize.

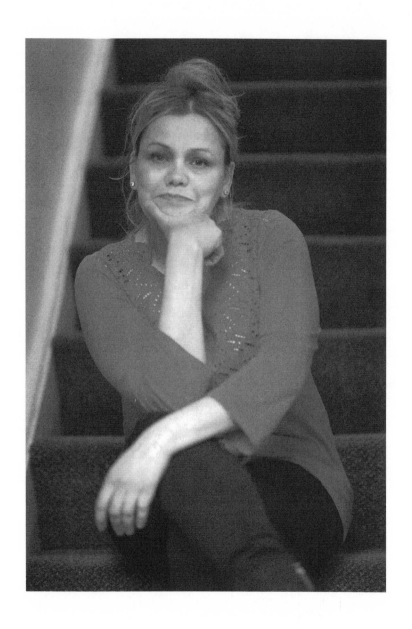

About the Author

Jillian's combination of compelling stories, humanitarian effort, and inspirational wisdom, always spellbind her audiences including Cambridge University, King's College London, Bank of England, McDonalds, Barclays, Nova Nordisk and countless others. She inspires her audiences to appreciate their potential and how to achieve it.

As a survivor of poverty and oppression, Jillian Haslam brings a unique perspective gained from decades of proven resilience. She uses her own story to show others how to derive meaning from their hardships, find grace in adversity, and develop genuine purpose to achieve their destiny. Jillian honors the invaluable story within us all and shows us how to integrate our darkest moments in order to light the way to fulfillment.

Born in the slums of Calcutta to parents of British ancestry, Jillian faced a bruising childhood of extreme poverty, malnutrition, and disease. But from a young age, she had a gift of seeing beauty among the grit. Despite the bleakest of circumstances, Jillian demonstrates the messages of hope, generosity, and community, which she uses to

achieve her own dreams today. Audiences leave inspired to face their own adversity and achieve their destiny.

Determined to reduce the number of people facing the same hardships as her, Jillian has launched charities to empower everyone from young children and women to the elderly and disadvantaged. Her tireless work has brought her a growing list of awards, including the Mother Teresa Memorial International Award, and The True Legend Award from *The Telegraph*. *The Independent* honoured her at the Asian Woman of the Year Awards.

When Jillian is not traveling on the public speaking circuit or working with her charities, she can be found at her home outside of London where she lives with her husband and their lovely Shih Tzu, Molly.

You can find more information about Jillian Haslam at the following links:

jillianhaslam.com

facebook.com/jillian.haslam

Twitter @jillianhaslam

IG @haslamjillian

LinkedIn jillianhaslam

remediatrust.org

Down But Not Out

A Paean for Jillian

I took all the body blows
the upper cuts
the left hooks that came my way
life never pulled any punches
I may hace buckled at the knees
but, I refused to be knocked out

let her throw her sucker punches
her huge haymakers to the jaw
I'll take these punches on the chin
when the countdown's almost ten
I'll rise once more from the ground
all set to fight again
I'll fight again
I'll fight the fight: win or lose
I'm ready for life's next round!

Neil Daswani, Author and Poet
June 30th 2022